Confidence of The Mob

The IRS Agent Who Took Down the Mafia — Then Advised Them

The Remarkable True Story of Fred G. Pastore

Confidence of The Mob: The IRS Agent Who Took Down the Mafia—Then Advised Them

First Edition: February 2026

ISBN - 979-8-9950804-0-4

Published in the United States of America

Visit the official website: ConfidenceofTheMob.com

Cover & Interior Design by Eddy Manfred Inserra III

Table of Contents

Dedication ....

Introduction ....

1. The Press Conference 1

2. East Boston 7

3. Boston Back Then 12

4. Investigations 30

5. Racket Squad 45

6. Patriarca Family Targets...52

7. Bernard Goldfine..59

8. JFK & RFK Target Fred...70

9. We're Going Into Business 100

10. Family, Friends, & FAMILY 117

11. 98 Prince Street 122

12. Fred's Final Years...128

13. Finding Millions of Dollars..139

14. Final Impact...147

15. References & Documents 157

Dedication

dy's little girl." They shared a rare bond: friendship, trust, and that unbreakable father-daughter connection. When my father died, I finally understood what my mother must have felt decades earlier, when she lost her dad when she was 30 years old. Now I knew the weight of that kind of loss.

I wanted to keep Fred's name and legacy alive. You won't find this story on Google. You won't see it in history books. But it's a story worth telling—and the least I could do is bring it into the light.

I dedicate this book to my mom, Sharman Inserra (Pastore)—thank you for the time we get to share and the love you give to my sons, little Eddy IV, and Andrew. I also dedicate this book to my Father Edward Inserra II, who instilled a "do it yourself" mentality in me at a young age, and showed me that you can change the world if you apply yourself. And finally I dedicate this to my Grandmother "Nana, Nina", Antonina Pastore (Cassetta).

Introduction

This story is real.

Every name, every event, every document, every photo, every twist—non-fiction.

You won't find it on Wikipedia. It's never been told.

But it's a missing piece of American history. A story of power, corruption, legacy, loyalty, and family.

My grandfather was Manfred Giacomo Pastore, known to most as Fred G. Pastore. Born on July 5, 1919. Died in 1988 from cancer (I was only 8 years old when he passed). He served as Group Supervisor of the **IRS Intelligence Division, Northeast District**—now known as the Criminal Investigation Unit. This was the same division that took down Al Capone.

Fred operated in New England during a time when the Italian Mafia was gaining real political power, gambling and the daily numbers were their revenue streams, when Eisenhower, and later JFK would become President, and when his brother Robert F. Kennedy was Attorney General.

Boston was the center of this storm—and Fred was smack in the middle of it.

Alongside this narrative, you'll find exclusive documents and photographs—many discovered in a dusty 50-year-old Florida oranges box that my Mother gave to me over 10 years ago. My Mother didn't know what was inside this box that she had in her attic since 1988. It was hundreds of documents, and from a quick glance, it looked like it was filled with accounting ledgers and boring pages of numbers. I didn't touch the box for months, I put it on top of my kitchen cabinets and forgot about it. One day, I decided to take a look inside the box. What I found, were IRS case notes and profiles of some of the biggest names in Boston Mafia and Underworld history. Names that you'd hear in the media in the 1990's-2000's, and names that Radio Personality and writer, Howie Carr would write books about. Names of characters in Hollywood movies, my jaw hit the floor. This wasn't a box full of accounting ledgers, it was my Grandfather's whole IRS career. Included in the box were IRS memos, Newspaper articles, Fred's personal journals, and even a telegram Fred sent directly to President Kennedy and Attorney General Bobby Kennedy.

Fred's investigations touched some of the biggest names in American organized crime and politics:

Raymond Patriarca, the Angiulo Brothers, Sherman Adams, President Dwight Eisenhower, John F. Kennedy, Robert Kennedy Sr, Bernard Goldfine, Frank Iaconi, Larry Zannino, Frank Salemme, Steve Flemmi, Peter Limone, and more.

Many of their names would later be tied to some of the most infamous trials and racketeering busts in U.S. history.

This story is also about government corruption at the highest levels—and how the system turned on Fred for doing his job too well. When he refused to be reassigned to a politically motivated demotion, they tried to bury him.

But Fred wasn't built to be buried.

He fought back—beginning with a pivotal press conference that would change his life, and the IRS forever. Fred had unwavering integrity, he refused to compromise. And when he walked away from the IRS, he walked straight into a new life:

as a tax advisor to some of the same people he used to investigate.

Fred understood the system better than anyone. He helped design some of the IRS's own investigative policies. And now, he was using that knowledge to protect his clients —legally—against the very agency that cast him aside.

You'll learn Fred's famous formula—$C + R = J$—which he used as a kind of north star in investigations. That formula still floats around IRS offices today.

To write this book and to create an audio podcast about this story, I conducted interviews with Fred's old colleagues, former IRS agents, family members, media experts, attorneys, even mafia figures. The story I'm telling is based on those interviews, the documents Fred left behind, and the impact his life had on everyone around him—including me.

My name is Eddy Inserra, and I'm Fred's grandson. I was born and raised in Woburn, Massachusetts, just ten minutes north of Boston. I'm an internet entrepreneur, and a subject matter expert in the X-ray detection space. I grew up in a house on a cul-de-sac with a basketball hoop, four siblings, and a lot of love. Fred was my mother's father. She and her sister Pamela were raised in Arlington, MA.

Fred's career had two acts:

First, as a rising star in the IRS Intelligence Unit, where he led some of the most important investigations in the country. And conducted the most comprehensive raids at the time, busting down doors, and taking down gambling dens.

The actual box that had Fred's documents inside and helped me figure out this story.

And second, as a private tax fraud consultant, serving powerful clients who once feared him. This is the story of how those two acts collided.

The title of this story came from a book in the 1970's by a man named "Vincent 'Fat Vinnie' Teresa". He was a member of the Patriarca crime family, and in one of his books he mentions a man who was a big hot shot at the IRS, then he retired, and that's when he made good money. *He could fix anything, and he had the **confidence of the mob.***

If you want to hear this story unfold with original audio clips from interviews of Fred's clients, media experts, friends, adversaries, and family, I've created a companion podcast about Fred's life. You'll also be able to access all of the documents in this book in high resolution, and you'll have access to photos, and other documents not provided in this book, but part of Fred's IRS files.

Just go to

ConfidenceofTheMob.com/Book

Or point your mobile device camera here to hear audio stories, interviews, and to see full size documents from this chapter.

SUBJECT: FRED G. PASTORE

SERVICE HISTORY: 1945 - 1962

1945
Appointed Special Agent, IRS Intelligence Division.

1951
Promoted to Acting Group Supervisor, Racket Squad. Begins
targeting major racketeers in New England.

1955
Named Group Supervisor. Spearheads the "Net Worth" method
to prosecute organized crime figures.

1958
Infiltrates Raytheon Manufacturing Co.; exposes widespread
gambling ring affecting national defense production.

1959
The Betrayal. IRS pressures Fred to lay off his
investigation into Bernard Goldfine against Pastore's
direct protests.

APRIL 1961
FBI Interrogation. Fred is questioned regarding alleged
bribes from targets. Allegations unfounded.

AUGUST 1961
The Guilio Incident. Confidential Informant (Family
Member) exposed during police stop; Pastore intervenes.

DEC 15, 1961
Resignation. Pastore leaves IRS; announcing Government
corruption and suspicious pressure from Attorney General
Bobby Kennedy and the U.S. President John F. Kennedy.

MARCH 1962
The Flip. FBI surveillance confirms Pastore is now
advising the Patriarca Crime Family among 100's of others
in need of his tax fraud advisory services.

Key Milestones in Fred G. Pastore's Career (1945–1962).

Key Players

(Real people in the Story)

Family

Fred G. Pastore

The fearless IRS agent who fought the mob, political corruption, and the government itself—and paid the price for his integrity.

Nina Pastore

Fred's loyal and loving wife, who stood by his side from the streets of East Boston to the mountains of New Hampshire.

Bobby Pastore

Fred's nephew, and the son of Fred's brother Giulio, a major contributor to the companion podcast.

Sharman Inserra (Pastore)

Fred's youngest daughter, and the emotional heartbeat of his family legacy.

Pamela Kennedy (Pastore)

Fred's eldest daughter, a constant support during his most public and private battles.

Sandy Kennedy

Son-in-law of Fred and Nina Pastore. Married to their daughter Pamela Pastore. Also worked for Fred at his tax advisory firm.

Fred Pastore (Nephew).

Fred's nephew, and brother of Bobby and Jimmy. Son of Fred's brother Giulio. A genius with numbers and the current owner of "Fred G. Pastore and Associates". Also Guinness book record holder.

Giulio Pastore

Fred's brother, and confidant, Bob and Fred Pastore Jr's Father. Husband to Rita Pastore.

Eddy Inserra II

Fred's trusted son-in-law, who cared for Fred during his final years and carried on his practical legacy.

The Trusted Allies

Frank DiMento

Former Assistant District Attorney turned Fred's legal hammer and closest professional ally in private practice.

Henry Vara

Boston nightlife kingpin—and Fred's first major private client after leaving the IRS.

Irwin Chafetz

One of Fred's first clients, Casino Mogul, and business partner of Sheldon Adelson.

The Adversaries and Power Players

Gennaro "Jerry" Angiulo

The North End's gambling king. Fred's cat-and-mouse adversary across decades of raids and quiet negotiations.

Bernard Goldfine

A textile tycoon whose secret favors and political connections would bring down some of the most powerful men in Washington.

Sherman Adams

President Eisenhower's Chief of Staff, toppled in the scandal Fred's investigation unearthed.

John F. Kennedy (JFK)

Massachusetts Senator turned President—his administration stood on the other side of Fred's battle for truth.

Robert F. Kennedy (RFK)

Attorney General. Tireless, ruthless—and determined to force Fred to reveal what he knew.

Frank Iaconi

Worcester mob boss who gave Fred the first thread that would unravel a national scandal.

Stephen "The Rifleman" Flemmi

One of Boston's most feared underworld figures, whose paths quietly crossed Fred's later in life.

The Battlegrounds

IRS Intelligence Unit

Fred's original command post—the sword and shield against America's financial criminal underground.

Patriarca Crime Family

New England's mafia dynasty—constantly at odds with Fred's raids and federal investigations.

Prince Street, Boston

Where cannoli was sold in the front—and empires were run in the back.

East Boston

Fred's childhood streets. Hard lessons. Harder victories.

North Conway, New Hampshire

The mountain retreat where Fred found brief peace in a world full of battles.

And the Secret That Changed Everything

The Box

<u>Sealed.</u> Forgotten. Buried under years of dust.

<u>Inside it:</u> the real story Fred Pastore refused to let die.

CHAPTER 1

The Press Conference

December 15, 1961

Federal Building, Boston, Massachusetts

Fred G. Pastore, Group Supervisor of the IRS Intelligence Division, Northeast District, stood at the podium in a packed press room. Flashbulbs popped. Reporters clutched notepads. Behind him, a typed copy of his speech sat on the podium, next to a small folded handkerchief. Fred's daughter Pamela, his mother-in-law, and his brother Giulio were seated off to the side. His wife, Nina, and youngest daughter, Sharman, were home sick with a winter cold.

Fred straightened his posture, cleared his throat, stared into the room, and began.

The IRS, he explained, had just informed him that he was being demoted—from his supervisory role in Boston to a Special Agent position in Syracuse, New York. The decision, he claimed, had nothing to do with performance and everything to do with politics.

He told the reporters that the demotion was orchestrated by officials high up the chain—including Attorney General Robert F. Kennedy and, perhaps, even President John F. Kennedy himself. He revealed that the FBI had opened a probe into his finances, based on information provided by two high-level criminal figures he'd recently helped convict. It was retaliation, he said. A smear campaign, designed to force him out.

Fred's speech was bold, precise, and unapologetic. He accused the government of punishing him for pursuing high-profile tax fraud cases too aggressively. Specifically, the case against textile magnate, Bernard Goldfine. He laid out his decades of service. He named names.

This wasn't a quiet resignation.

This was a war cry.

Outside the federal building, newspapers were already preparing their headlines. Inside, Fred gave his last official address as an IRS agent.

By the end of the press conference, one thing was missing, Fred didn't reveal the names of politicians and police officers in Boston who were "on the take," like he promised he would. The press and media expected Fred to reveal them, he didn't, it was Fred's insurance policy, he kept them in his back pocket.

What few knew then—but what this book will reveal—is that Fred wasn't just stepping down. He was stepping into a new chapter—one that would flip the entire city of Boston and the IRS upside down.

Official UPI Press photos from the newspaper headlines, of Fred's resignation from the IRS.

Access high resolution scans of Fred's speech, press clippings and other documents here:

ConfidenceofTheMob.com/book

*Or point your mobile device
camera here to hear audio
stories, interviews, and to
see full size documents from
this chapter.*

Fred G. Pastore's press release that went out stating he was resigning from the IRS.

December 15, 1961

The following Statement by Fred G. Pastore is released for general publication:

After twenty and one-half years of Government Service, I have resigned from the Internal Revenue Service effective December 15, 1961, rather than accept a transfer to other duties at Syracuse, New York, because I believe that in view of my record such reassignment was not made for the good of the Service and was entirely unfair to me.

I leave the Internal Revenue Service with a completely clear conscience and the satifaction of knowing, without any reservation of any kind, that I have at all times, without exception, performed my duties and conducted myself in the best interestsof the Internal Revenue Service and of the United States Government.

For me to accept a transfer to Syracuse to a non-supervisory position would result in my not being able to acquire the necessary administratrive experience to qualify me for further advancement in the Internal Revenue Service.

I am proud of my work and results obtained in the Bernard Goldfine investigation and in the racketeer and wagering tax areas.

I thank all of the Special and Revenue Agents, the clerical and stenographic staff and all others in the Internal Revenue Service who co-operated with me during the same.

Page 1 of 2.

Fred G. Pastore's press release that went out stating he was resigning from the IRS.

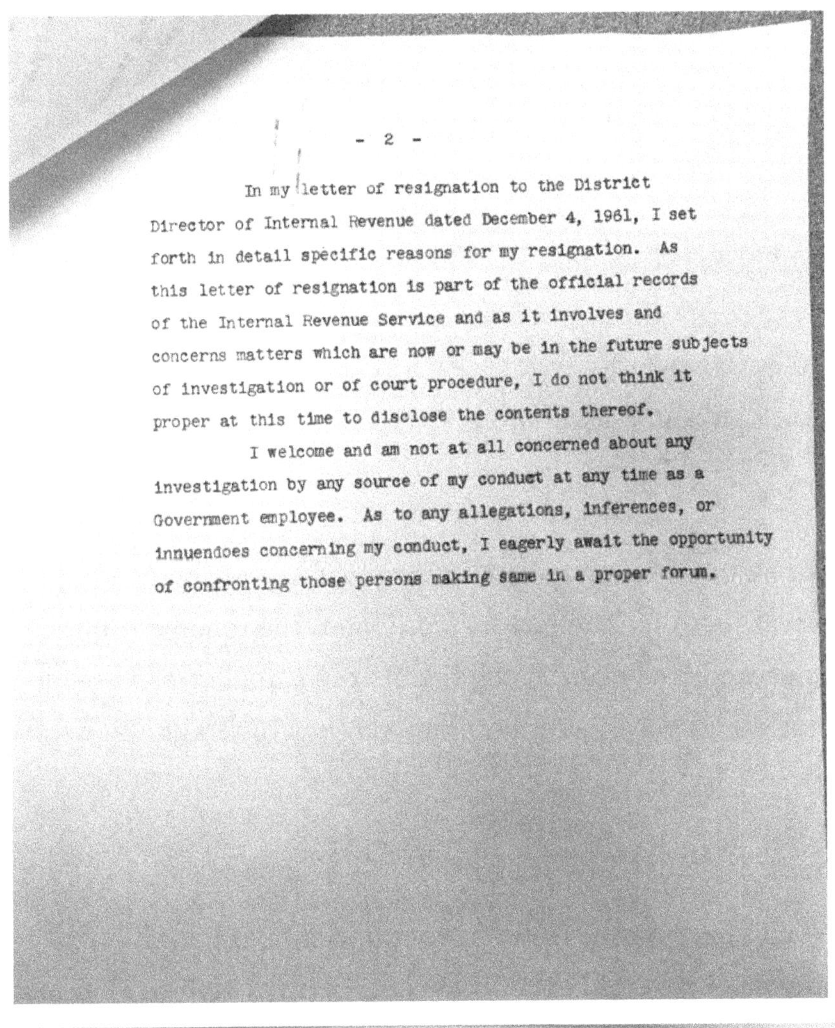

- 2 -

In my letter of resignation to the District Director of Internal Revenue dated December 4, 1961, I set forth in detail specific reasons for my resignation. As this letter of resignation is part of the official records of the Internal Revenue Service and as it involves and concerns matters which are now or may be in the future subjects of investigation or of court procedure, I do not think it proper at this time to disclose the contents thereof.

I welcome and am not at all concerned about any investigation by any source of my conduct at any time as a Government employee. As to any allegations, inferences, or innuendoes concerning my conduct, I eagerly await the opportunity of confronting those persons making same in a proper forum.

Page 2 of 2.

CHAPTER 2

East Boston

Before he was "Mr. Pastore," before the press conferences and the mafia clients, before the IRS badge and the gold-lettered desk placard—Fred G. Pastore was just a poor skinny Italian kid from East Boston.

He grew up in a time when poverty wasn't whispered about —it was just life. The streets were loud, the tenement buildings packed, and every block had its own smell: fresh bread, motor oil, garlic, or sewage—depending which way the wind blew.

Fred and his brother Giulio (pronounced JOO-lee-oh) would steal coal off of the local train in order to heat their home. At Christmas time, there was no tree, there were no gifts. That's how tight things were.

During summers, he'd sell watermelons off the back of a truck, barking the famous melodic *Watermeeeeelllooooon!* And prices at passersby on the corner of Porter and Maverick. On Saturdays, he and his brother would scrape together a nickel and head to the movie theater. One ticket, one seat. They'd split it—literally. One sat on the other's lap.

But even then, Fred had something different in him—a sharpness. A way of reading people. A memory that never failed. His family saw it too.

His sisters, his mother, even his father, who rarely praised anyone, believed Fred had the brains to make it out of the neighborhood. They made sacrifices so he could go to school, buy books, take night classes. The family didn't talk about dreams. They worked for them.

It was around this time that Fred met Nina, the woman who would become his wife. She was beautiful, sharp, and tough in her own way. They met young—teenagers really—and by the time they were in their early twenties, they were married.

The ceremony was small, simple. A few friends, some family. Air raid sirens screamed overhead during the vows—it was wartime, after all—but Fred barely flinched. He looked into Nina's eyes and promised her a future far removed from the streets they grew up on.

Fred had one childhood friend from the East Boston neighborhood, they were with each other all the time. His name was Guy Spagnuolo. Nina grew up at 241 Princeton Street in East Boston. Fred grew up on 142 Porter Street, and Fred's childhood friend grew up on 40 Princeton Street. So, Nina and Guy grew up on the same street. They were all East Boston kids, and East Boston helped mold them to have that street grit and confidence in the future. There was also another kid who was born the same year as Fred and Guy, both in 1919, and they grew up knowing each other as well. His name was Gennaro "Jerry" Angiulo.

One thing that people said that Fred and Guy would say when anyone would bring up Jerry later on in life, they'd say "yeah, we knew the Angiulo brothers growing up", "you had two choices in those days, you could go down the path we went, or you could go down the path Jerry and his brothers went, but we all came from the same place." Remember Jerry's name, we will talk about him later in the book.

Fred's family leaned in to support him. The Pastore clan wasn't perfect, but when they believed in something—or someone—they backed them all the way. Fred's sisters worked overtime, and his brothers picked up extra shifts, just to help pay for Fred's education. There were five of them all together, two girls and three boys. They knew he

9

was their shot. The one who could carry the family name out of East Boston and into something bigger.

Fred didn't waste it.

He studied like a machine—law, accounting, procedure, taxation. Anything that could move him forward. He graduated from Northeastern University, and then attended MIT as well. He took the civil service exam and scored near the top. When he got the letter offering him a position with the Internal Revenue Service, he knew this was the beginning of everything he had worked toward.

But even as he put on a suit and started carrying a badge, Fred never forgot East Boston.

He still walked those streets. Still stopped in the old barber shop for a trim. Still tipped the kids selling newspapers on the corner. He wore the IRS badge, yes. But under it all, he still had that Eastie fire. That chip on the shoulder. That unspoken promise that he would never let anyone—government or gangster—push him around. My cousin Bobby Pastore (Fred's nephew), says his father Giulio and Fred had "True Grit", from being "tough guys" in the neighborhood growing up. Fred and Giulio also had an unbreakable bond. Giulio was the quiet one who didn't really stand out, and saw everything, but said nothing. You could meet Giulio, and forget him within a minute. Fred was the one who took action. After you met Fred, he made an impression, you wouldn't forget him.

Giulio would later go on to be in the military, and when he came back, he was a traveling housewares salesman. Usually gone all day or sometimes days at a time on the road.

Fred's daughter Pamela Kennedy (Pastore) says, in Fred's neighborhood growing up, you could either go this way (pointing to her left), or you could go this way (pointing to her right), and Fred decided to go this way (the right). She meant back then, in the Italian neighborhood you could go down the path of being a hoodlum, or you could go down the "honest" path and pursue a job or career, what many would consider the right way to go.

Fred may have left the old neighborhood behind.

But it never left him.

CHAPTER 3

Boston Back Then

To understand Fred's work, you need to understand the city.

Boston in the 1940s through the early 1960s was a living paradox—a city of tradition and transformation, law and lawlessness, working-class struggle and elite corruption. The skyline was different back then, before the Big Dig and the Seaport boom. But the real changes were in the streets and alleys, the neighborhoods that shaped the city's power players.

East Boston and the North End were home to the Italian families. Tight-knit, traditional, and territorial. Walk a block off Hanover Street and you'd find basement card games, cash-only storefronts, and old men on stoops whispering about "insurance policies" that had nothing to do with health care.

Fred G. Pastore (Left) & Guy Spagnuolo (Right) in their
late teenage years, with big dreams
(Photo is Courtesy of Virginia Spagnuolo Hennessey)

Nina and Fred on right at Revere Beach taking a photo.

WED AS RAID SIRENS WAIL

East Boston Couple First to Do So

With the wail of sirens echoing through the Church of Our Lady of Mt. Carmel, East Boston, Miss Antonina Cassetta of 217 Princeton street, that district, became the bride of Manfred Pastore of 142 Porter street at a wedding ceremony performed yesterday during the air raid test. The Rev. Henry Borrelli officiated.

Attired in a gown of white satin with lace veil and coronet, and carrying a bouquet of lilies of the valley, the bride marched to the altar as the sirens almost drowned out the traditional wedding march. Following the ceremony they were given a reception at the home of the bride's parents and later left for a trip to New York.

Fred and Nina's unique wedding in East Boston.

Fred and Nina

Southie was Irish turf—tough, proud, and prone to brawls.

Roxbury and Mattapan were predominantly Black neighborhoods, pushing against segregation and economic barriers.

Dorchester and Brookline had thriving Jewish communities, family businesses, and a growing professional class.

This wasn't a melting pot.

It was a patchwork of tribes, each with their own rules.

And if you were smart? You learned how to navigate between them.

Fred's IRS badge gave him authority. But it was his street smarts, sharp instincts, and sheer presence that made him effective. He didn't just understand tax code—he understood people. He knew that some bar owners had to rig a pinball machine just to make rent. But he also knew when someone was running a front for a much bigger operation.

And pinball machines were just the beginning.

Pinball Machines & Pocket Money

17

Back then, coin-operated pinball machines were everywhere—diners, barbershops, pizza joints. They weren't just for fun. Most of them were rigged for gambling, and many establishments were making serious untaxed cash on the side.

That put them in Fred's crosshairs.

He led dozens of coordinated raids across Massachusetts, targeting these illegal gambling operations. Some were mom-and-pop shops trying to survive. Others were controlled by known racketeers, laundering gambling money through vending routes and jukebox services.

This map was inside the box, it showed some of the locations Fred would raid at the time.

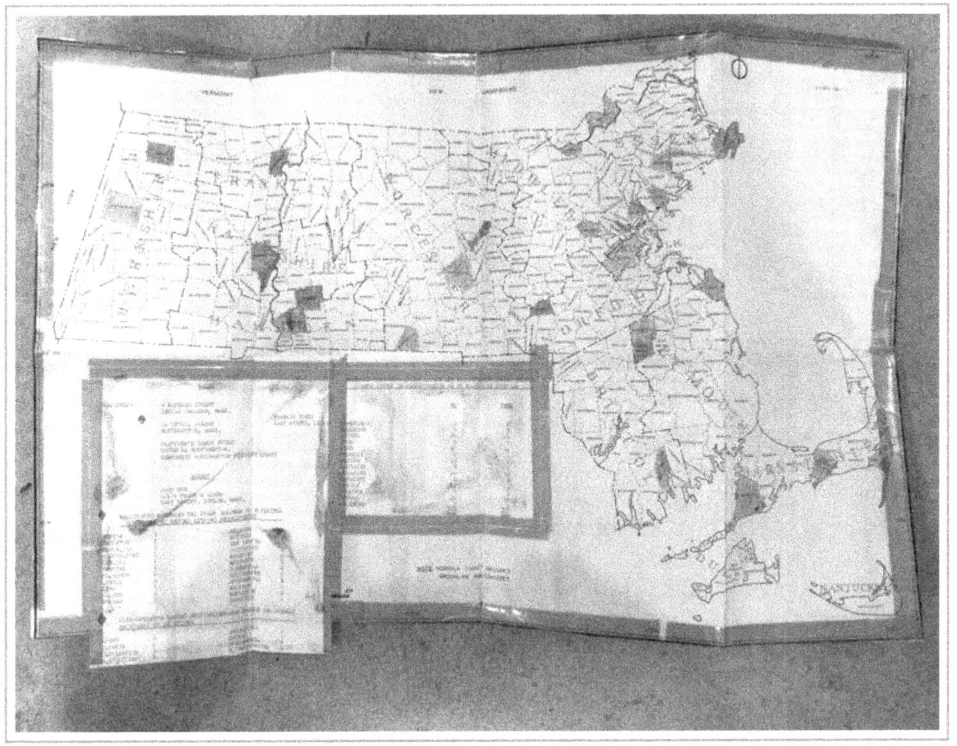

The Racket Hierarchy

Fred wasn't just busting machines. He was building profiles—files, charts, and behavioral bios—on the men behind them.

He kept notes in his signature tight script, categorizing their activities:

- Gambling
- Loan sharking
- Smuggling
- Bookmaking
- Racketeering
- Tax evasion

Fred knew who fronted for whom, who handled collections, who controlled which corners of the vending routes. He understood the power pyramid—not from wiretaps, but from old-school legwork, observation, and math.

The following documents are Fred's original typewritten profiles of New England's suspected most notorious racketeers in 1961, listing names, known aliases, affiliated businesses, suspected income streams, IRS code violations, and notes from field surveillance. These internal records would later be used in joint investigations with state police and FBI, Fred's work is even mentioned in the JFK assassination files when they were investigating someone in Boston potentially connected to the event.

Fred (right) answering bookie calls during a bust.

<u>The names are listed below (spelled as-is in the documents):</u>

1. Freddie Angiullo

2. Nicola Ghisi

3. Dominic Isabella

4. Leventhal

5. Tony Sandrelli

6. Tony Santaniello

7. Nicholas C. Camerota

8. Samuel Cufari

9. Bernard McGarry

10. Elliot Price

11. Francis Santo

12. Abraham Sarkis

13. Francis Sullivan

14. Raymond Patriarca

15. Samuel Rosencranz

16. Nick Angiullo

17. Walter "Wimpy" Bennett

18. Larry Bioni aka Illario Zannino - <u>Continued</u>...

Fred's document titled "Evaluation of Names of Possible Racketeers in the Boston District."

I:D

Boston, Massachusetts
March 10, 1961

MEMORANDUM TO: Chief, Intelligence Division

In re: Evaluation of Names of Possible
Racketeers in the Boston District

You recently gave me a list of names of persons reputed to be racketeers in the Boston District and asked me to evaluate their illegal status.

The files of the Intelligence Division disclose no record of the following individuals:

> Angiullo, Freddie
> Ghisi, Nicòla
> Isabella, Dominic
> Leventhal
> Sandrelli, Tony
> Santaniello, Tony

On the current Major Racketeer list are the following individuals and a biographical sketch was submitted to you on each under memorandum dated March 2, 1961:

> Camerota, Nicholas C.
> Cufari, Samuel
> Lombardo, Joseph
> McGarry, Bernard
> Price, Elliot
> Santo, Francis
> Sarkis, Abraham
> Sullivan, Francis

<u>Patriarca, Raymond</u>

This name also appeared on the list furnished to me. Patriarca is a Rhode Island taxpayer and he is generally reputed to control a substantial part of illegal wagering and enforcement of gambling debts in the New England area.

In re: Evaluation of ⟨ ⟩s of Possible
        Racketeers i⟨ ⟩ Boston District

Samuel Rosencranz is reputed to be engaged mainly in the financing of illegal stills. However, since at least December 1960 he has operated a major bookmaking and lottery operation at 584 Beach Street, Revere, Massachusetts. This location was raided by federal agents on February 27, 1961 and Rosencranz, present at the time of the raid, was not arrested as there was no arrest warrant outstanding in his name. He is the owner of a 1960 Cadillac which was seized during the raid for being used in violation of Section 7302 of the Internal Revenue Code of 1954. Rosencranz stated that he has not filed income tax returns since 1956 and he does not hold a Wagering Occupational Tax stamp.

His name will be added to the Major Racketeer list and he is currently being investigated for the two offenses(wagering occupational tax and failure to file).

Biographical sketches of the remaining persons on the list furnished me are as follows:

Angiullo, Nick

The last income tax investigation of this taxpayer was in 1958 and covered the years 1955, 1956 and 1957. His 1957 income tax return disclosed an adjusted gross income of $25,101.25, described as a salary from a local cafe of $10,400.00 and gratuities of $14,701.25.

In my opinion, this individual is a bookmaker but not of such notoriety as to be included in the Major Racketeer list.

Bennett, Walter

The file concerning this individual is in the Archives and will not be available until Monday, March 13, 1961.

Bioni, Larry, a/k/a Ilario Zannino

This individual is currently being investigated by Special Agent Morrell S. Edgerly. He is associated with Leo Santaniello and Philip Waggenheim, all of whom are now serving state sentences for extorting money from a legitimate business man.

Zannino, Waggenheim and Santaniello are also loan sharks and strong arm men for the syndicate enforcing gambling debts.

The name of Santaniello has appeared in the bookmaking records seized at the home of Carmello Coco during Operation Cedar in April 1960.

- 2 -

Fred's document titled "Evaluation of Names of Possible Racketeers in the Boston District."

In re: Evaluation of Names of Possible
         Racketeers in the Boston District

Buccola, Philip

This taxpayer has been repeatedly investigated by the Intelligence Division without success. A large part of his income is derived from dividends of Wonderland Park, Revere, Massachusetts. He is in Italy most of the time but makes periodic visits to Boston. He is reputed to be second in command in the New England area under Raymond Patriarca of Rhode Island.

Callanan, Timmy

A wagering occupational tax investigation was conducted on this individual for fiscal year ending June 30, 1960, by the Intelligence Division without success. Although his source of income on his tax returns was listed as profits from juke box and pinball machines, it is suspected that he is a major factor in controlling wagering and enforcement of gambling debts in the South Boston area.

Cesario, Sal

This individual was the subject of a wagering occupational tax investigation for the year 1959 without success. He currently operates a TV and radio repair shop in the South End section and a consent search was made of these premises by federal agents and the Boston Police in September 1960. No evidence of wagering was found. It is my opinion that Cesario is a minor element in this area.

David, Watty

This individual is reputed to be a narcotics peddler and distributor and hangs around the South End area. It is believed that he plays a major part in the receiving and distributing of narcotics.

Ferrara, Francis

This individual operated a major racing results center on Summer Street, Boston, under the name of Sportsday Weekly. He recently was sent to prison in connection with stolen government bonds and the business of racing results was taken over by Angelo Rossetti. Ferrara is still in prison.

Page 3 of 5.

Fred's document titled "Evaluation of Names of Possible ble Racketeers in the Boston District."

In re: Evaluation of Names of Possible
         Racketeers in the Boston District

<u>Fox, Louis</u>

It is generally rumored that this individual exercises a considerable
amount of behind-the-scenes influence in the racket activities in
Revere. No definite evidence has been established to connect this
individual with illegal activities.

<u>Lamartino, Ralph "Ching Chong"</u>

This individual is believed to be a small bookmaker and hangs around
the Messina Restaurant, Commercial Street, Boston. He is also known
as "Chong" and is a very effective knife wielder, according to my
information. He is reputed to be a loan shark and strong arm man in
enforcing gambling debts.

<u>LaMorte, Michael, alias "Big Mike" Morelli</u>

This taxpayer has been investigated by the Intelligence Division and
was convicted for violation of the Wagering Tax Statutes on May 3,
1955. He was sentenced to six(6) months in jail and fined $1,000.
Currently, the best available information is that he operates a dice
and card game. I think he is an influential figure in this area.

<u>Palladino, Rocco</u>

During the Racketeer Drive in 1951, an income tax investigation of
this taxpayer resulted in a recommendation that he be prosecuted for
tax evasion. The Grand Jury returned a no bill. It is believed that
Palladino is an influential figure in the rackets, but is presently
engaged in a shylock operation and not in any form of wagering.

<u>Sagansky, Harry "Doc"</u>

This taxpayer, together with Louis Fox, reports income from legitimate
sources, which exceeds $100,000 a year. Sagansky was arrested in 1954
by the Brookline Police for violation of local gambling statutes and
recommendation was made that he be prosecuted for violation of the
Federal Wagering Tax Statutes. However, the District Court judge, at
the conclusion of the presentation of the government's evidence, approved
a motion filed by defense counsel and directed that he be found not
guilty. Since 1954 no definite evidence has been uncovered by any law
enforcement agency that Sagansky is engaged in any illegal activities.

- 4 -

Page 4 of 5.

In re: Evaluation of Names of Possible
          Racketeers in the Boston District

<u>Sagansky, Harry "Doc"(cont.)</u>

Nevertheless, it is believed he is an influential figure in wagering operations and that he possibly finances other bookmakers and that he is a big sports operator in this area.

<u>Visconte, Robert L.</u>

This taxpayer was also investigated by the Intelligence Division as a result of being involved in illegal activities, but without success. It is believed he is a minor figure in the rackets and not worthy of extensive investigation.

<u>Williams, Johnny "Guillermo"</u>

This taxpayer was investigated for Wagering Tax violations for fiscal year 1959 without success. His income tax returns disclosed income from a juke box business. He hangs around Giro's Cafe on Hanover Street, in Boston, which is owned and operated by a major racketeer, Joseph Lombardo. The best available information at this time is that he is engaged in bookmaking and is also a strong arm man for a local group enforcing gambling debts.

His income tax return for the year 1957 disclosed an item of income in the amount of $15,000 which was earned at the Tropicana Club in Havana, Cuba. The taxpayer produced a receipt to show the money received for services rendered in connection with public relations in the United States. The taxpayer said that he earned the money originally for the promoting and playing of Bingo at the Tropicana Club in 1957. It was not possible to obtain verification at that time because of political conditions in Cuba.

FRED G. PASTORE
Group Supervisor

19.   Philip Buccola

20.   Tommy Callahan

21.   Sal Cesario

22.   Watty David

23.   Francis Ferrara

24.   Louis Fox

25.   Ralph "Ching Chong" Lamartino

26.   Michael "Big Mike Morelli" LaMorte

27.   Rocco Palladino

28.   Harry "Doc" Sagansky

29.   Robert L. Visconte

30.   Johnny "Guillermo" Williams

These are the "Who's who" of the criminal underworld and gambling operations in New England at that time. You have seen these names in movies, books, posts online, but this is the other side of the aisle, where you get to see the man who was investigating all of them for not paying their taxes from their illegal income.

This document has never been made public until now, I have a box full of documents that dive into these names and much more. I'm not going to walk through all the names and their bio's in this book. If you want to learn more about them you can find plenty of books by Howie Carr and others. One thing you will notice is that the main name that you usually see associated with Boston Mob stories from the time period isn't mentioned, Whitey Bulger. Whitey didn't care about paying taxes, most of his income was from illegitimate sources from businesses in other peoples names, tribute payments, or strong arming businesses. He wasn't on Fred's radar, and he didn't have to be, he was more of a gangster, not a mafia member, bookmaker, etc. Uncle Sam didn't care about Whitey not paying his taxes.

What made Fred dangerous to organized crime wasn't just that he could build a case. It was that he could build an entire operational blueprint.

He saw patterns. He saw how money moved.

He knew when the bar in Chelsea was a front for the club in Lynn, which was connected to a truck route in Fitchburg, and how all of it tied back to a guy on Prince Street with a cash counting machine in his basement.

Most lawmen saw only the tax returns.

Fred saw the ecosystem.

And he wasn't afraid to shine a light on it.

CHAPTER 4

Investigations

Fred didn't carry a weapon to feel powerful. He carried it because his job required it.

The IRS Intelligence Division wasn't just pushing paper. They were a law enforcement agency—with badges, sidearms, surveillance ops, and jurisdiction that could shake the foundation of legitimate businesses and criminal empires alike. They couldn't make arrests themselves, but their partners in the U.S. Marshals, FBI, and state and local police could—and Fred knew exactly how to coordinate the dance.

And when Fred led an investigation, it wasn't just a case—it was a mission.

The Intelligence Division (now called the Criminal Investigations Unit), are an elite group tasked with going after the biggest tax offenders. Elmer Irey and Elliot Ness were part of the foundation of this unit. Fred was one of them. And he was great at it.

The Raytheon Raid

One of Fred's earliest—and boldest—operations involved the Raytheon Manufacturing Corporation, a company that would later become a cornerstone of the U.S. military-industrial complex. But at the time, Raytheon had a problem. And it wasn't missiles or radar systems.

<u>It was gambling.</u>

In multiple Raytheon plants across Massachusetts, internal productivity was dropping, morale was dipping, and supervisors were reporting suspicious behavior in break rooms and bathrooms. Something was off. There were literally missile parts sitting on the production line while none of the workers were at their stations for hours at a time.

That's when Raytheon's Chief Financial Officer quietly reached out to the IRS.

Fred was assigned to lead the investigation. And instead of just combing through financial statements, Fred did what most wouldn't dare—he went inside.

He handpicked a team of undercover agents who applied for real jobs at Raytheon—some as janitors, others as line workers. They passed background checks. They showed up for orientation. He did this so his undercover agents wouldn't just get inserted into jobs without going through the normal process, as they didn't want to tip off anyone. The assumed gamblers were entrenched and had eyes everywhere. Fred's agents put on uniforms. And then they started watching and listening.

Weeks passed before the first breakthrough.

In the men's bathroom of one of the main plants, one of Fred's agents spotted a quiet exchange—a folded paper, a code word, a payout. It happened again the next day. Then again. The mens bathrooms had long lines all day long, because they were all placing bets for the daily number and sport betting in the bathroom stalls with the bookies! Eventually, a full system was uncovered: an internal gambling ring operating within the plant, at multiple facilities, collecting numbers and wagers during working hours.

The real danger?

This wasn't just some after-hours poker. These were production facilities for military technology—missiles and guidance systems being built for the Cold War effort. And the gambling ring was distracting the workforce, delaying production, and compromising national readiness.

Fred's operation broke the case wide open.

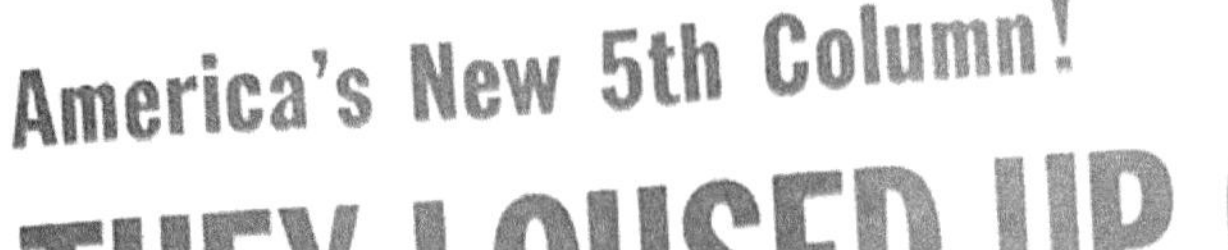

By

IF THE RUSSIANS had planned it, they c
hamper our defense program more effectivel
America's newest 5th Column is doing. The
ous, 1958-style saboteurs are the thousands of ga
who infest our military plants across the naiton.

Treasury agents, worried by the hold these rac
have on our defense workers, were powerless to a
recently. Now it looks as if a major crackdown is
nent.

The Federal hell that awaits the mobsters was
led by recent raids that smashed a multi-million
gambling ring operating in defense plants near l
There, T-men cleaned out a nest of bookies wl
actually held back production of one of the l
crack guided missiles.

To understand this shocking story, recall that last
January, Senate Majority Leader Lyndon Johnson com-
pleted a lengthly investigation of our lagging missile and
satellite programs by bluntly declaring:

"We are losing the race for survival!"

There are a lot of reasons for the mess we're in, but
one of them became clear just a week after Johnson's
warning. It was then that T-men swooped down on de-

"Bookies are wors
than Reds," say
Judge William McCarth
as T-Men crack
gambling rings in
our missile plants.

official said that "production of guided missiles was
seriously impeded."

In desperation, the company turned to the Treasury
Department, which immediately set up a task force of
Intelligence agents. These undercover operatives quickly
discovered that a lot of telephone calls were being made
from Raytheon and other U.S. defense plants to a gambling ring in Canada.

When the T-men realized (Continued on page 90)

"THE GAMBLING RING INSIDE RAYTHEON" — from
Confidential Magazine, 1954

Full-page spread highlighting the IRS Intelligence Division's investigation into Raytheon, led by Fred G. Pastore. The article warns of the national security risk posed by internal corruption and applauds the IRS's "innovative and undercover" approach to white-collar crime prevention.

Fred was praised in internal Treasury memos and even featured in National press. It was one of the first times his name showed up not just in government files—but in bold type on newsstands.

You can view the full size PDF article on our website, it's a great story to read.

The Frank Iaconi Trial

Fred's career wasn't built on luck—it was built on momentum.

Fresh off the Raytheon case, he was pulled into another investigation, the Brinks robbery. It was a daring midday robbery right at the Brinks Building in the North End of Boston, where robbers made away with$2.8 million dollars worth of cash and other securities. The robbery happened in

1950 but law enforcement had been chasing leads for years with no success.

Why did Fred get pulled into the bank robbery case, if it had nothing to do with tax revenue? Well, the FBI was investigating a man named Frank Iaconi. He was the reputed mob boss of Worcester, Massachusetts. He was part of the Genovese crime family, one of the five families from New York. They called him "The Gambling Czar". The Genovese territory came up to Springfield, and Worcester Massachusetts, but anything east of that was the local Patriarca Italian Mafia territory. During the FBI's interrogation, Iaconi said "I had nothing to do with that robbery, **I'm only a bookmaker!**".

Now, when Iaconi admitted to being a bookmaker, that alone would put him on the IRS' radar, but the FBI was run by J. Edgar Hoover. Hoover didn't want FBI mingling in cases to do with the IRS. So his FBI team walked away from Iaconi, and Fred and his IRS team were up next.

Iaconi ran the city of Worcester with an iron grip—bookmaking, bribery, loans, labor rackets. And he kept a relatively low profile for a man with so much power. But what drew Fred's attention wasn't just the activity—it was the money.

The IRS suspected that Iaconi wasn't reporting the vast majority of his income, and Fred was brought into build the financial case to put some pressure on Iaconi.

It didn't take long.

Fred traced income from Iaconi's club back to shell companies, then back to vending machine routes, then to real estate holdings under a maze of relatives' names. Iaconi knew he was about to get the hammer dropped on him, so he made a plea to Fred. He said "Fred, I've got information about a man who's got more power and influence than any street guy could ever have. I mean he's playing at a different level". Fred decided to hear Iaconi out, Iaconi hoped Fred would back down after he gave him a tip in good faith.

HEADED INVESTIGATION

Fred G. Pastore of Arlington Heights, Internal Revenue Service agent who headed the investigation of Frank Iaconi, goes over the books of corporations associated with Iaconi in testimony yesterday in Federal Court, Boston.

Iaconi

Continued from Page One

time in examination and cross examination, three agents of the eight sworn in Tuesday have

Fred is featured in a column highlighting
his work on the Iaconi case.

Fred got what he wanted from Iaconi, but Iaconi went to trial, and within 5 days, changed his plea from not-guilty, to guilty, thanks to Fred going on the stand in the case.

A story that one of Fred's colleagues, Francis "Frank" J. DiMento, who was at the District Attorney's office at the time says is "I saw Iaconi and Fred in the corridor in the court house, Iaconi said to Fred in his Italian/English accent "Hello, ah, Mr. Pastore", and Fred kept walking and replied "Goodbye Mr. Iaconi!". And Fred meant it, cause he went to jail right after that." This is where you see some of that street grit, and toughness, and even cockiness come out of Fred.

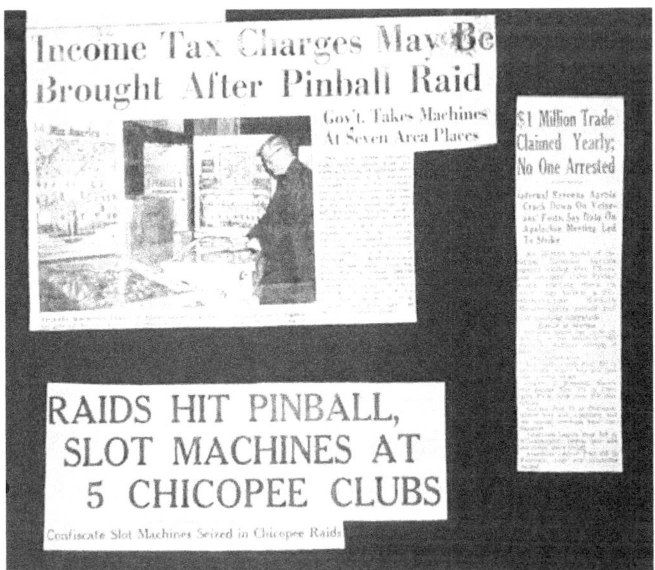

Pinball machines were a big source of income
that could be avoided paying taxes on easily.

The famous Mafia "Apalachin National Mafia Boss Meeting" was mentioned in this article in this gambling bust by Fred and his team in Revere, Massachusetts.

(Courtesy of Pamela Pastore, Fred's eldest daughter)

Fred had never heard the name that Iaconi gave him before. But once he did, it started showing up everywhere—on checks, on contracts, even in social circles that overlapped with political power players.

It would take months to unravel. But this was the first breadcrumb.

SCENE OF HUGE BOOKIE RAID IN EAST BOSTON NEAR MAVERICK SQ.

Fred and his team conducted some crucial raids en East Boston in 1959. This one in East Boston at Bartolo's Ringside Cafe, right across from the local police station, which set up a media battle between Fred and the police.

Trial Date Set for 13 In E. Boston Bet Raids

The 13 alleged bookies arrested in two East Boston raids last October by Federal agents were ordered to stand trial on April 18 by Judge George C. Sweeney in Federal Court yesterday.

All defendants pleaded not guilty to charges of violation of the Federal Wagering Tax Law in that they failed to register as bookies and failed to purchase an occupational stamp from the Internal Revenue Bureau.

Asst. U.S. Atty. Arlyne F. Hassett argued a motion to consolidate the cases, stating that the defendants were involved in a joint venture and that the evidence is intertwined.

She said that all the defendants had betting slips in their possession when Fred G. Pastore, group supervisor of the Intelligence Division of the Internal Revenue Service, swooped down on two locations in East Boston.

The motion to consolidate was opposed by defense attorneys Frank J. DiMento, Thomas W. Lawless and John H. Fitzgerald.

Defense lawyers were given five days in which to file special pleas.

The motion to consolidate was taken under advisement.

Raids were made at Bartolo's Ringside Cafe, Sumner st. and Chick's Bargain Shoe Store, Meridian and Havre, East Boston.

The unique aspect of the East Boston raids that Fred was working on was that Frank DiMento had started his own law practice and Fred and Frank were on opposite sides of this case.

And Fred knew exactly how to follow it.

As Fred's nephew, Fred Pastore Jr recalled "pinball machines didn't have flippers on them originally, so they were considered gambling machines, once they added the flippers, it became a game of skill, not a game of luck". That's why pinball machines have flippers on them today. Fun fact.

A New Kind of Investigator

Fred wasn't flashy. He didn't shout or wave his badge around.

He listened more than he spoke. He carried a notepad at all times. He read contracts like novels and bank records like diaries. He had a near photographic memory for numbers, dates, and names. And when he built a case, he built it from the foundation up—airtight and impossible to argue.

He ran his unit like a field operation, not a desk job. His team conducted surveillance, posed as civilians, interviewed whistleblowers in diners, and matched irregularities across thousands of pages of financial records without a single spreadsheet.

This was what made Fred dangerous:

He wasn't just building cases. He was building systems of truth.

And when people saw his name at the bottom of a report, they knew:

They were going to get nailed.

Fred always seemed to have the leg up on the racketeers. Like he had someone helping him, he knew where the bookies stashed their slips, he knew where they stowed their cash, he knew the players, he knew the game. It seemed too easy at times.

Fred did have a secret weapon. One that would not be uncovered until I pieced together some clues on my own, with documents from the box. And some help from my second cousins Bob Pastore, and Fred Pastore Jr.

We dive into this later.

Fred in the white trench coat burning gambling/betting slips during a raid.

Fred on the right with two of his IRS agents raiding Kelly's Sports Bar in Boston, July 14th 1960

CHAPTER 5

Racket Squad

Fred G. Pastore was no longer just an agent.

By the late 1950s, he had become a symbol—of accountability, precision, and quiet power inside one of the most feared agencies in the country.

His cases weren't just making headlines.

They were reshaping how the IRS Intelligence Unit operated in the field.

Fred wasn't reacting to crime. He was hunting it down before it made the news.

The Rise of the Racket Squad

In Boston and across New England, the underground economy was thriving—gambling rings, numbers games, loan sharking, unreported income from bars, strip clubs, trucking companies, vending machine monopolies, and everything in between. Most of it was invisible on paper. But Fred knew where to look.

He headed up the a newly created local division of a task force within the IRS that would focus specifically on large scale racketeers, informally dubbed "The Racket Squad," comprised of trusted agents from his district who could follow money like bloodhounds. The IRS placed "Racket Squad's" in key cities throughout the Nation. There was even a hit TV show with the same title at the time.

The squad would cross-reference license applications with tax filings, track currency movements between banks, and partner with local law enforcement—while always maintaining federal jurisdiction. This was a directive encouraged by Senator Estes Kefauver as he was running for President and he had what they called "Crime Hearings" in front of the Senate where they would call alleged mafia leaders in to question them on TV. You can see these on Youtube, they are great footage.

Each raid was a symphony:

Multiple locations.

Coordinated timing.

Seizure protocols.

Legal cover.

Media strategy.

And Fred conducted it all—clipboard in one hand, badge in the other.

The Headlines Begin

Fred's operations were so successful—and so dramatic—that the press took notice.

Local newspapers were tipped off about early morning busts.

Photographers were invited to photograph seized gambling equipment, stacks of money, and agents with badges raised in low-lit warehouses.

Fred's face began appearing regularly in print—stern, suit-clad, calm in the middle of chaos. They called Fred **"The Eliot Ness of Boston"**.

These weren't just petty gambling arrests. Fred's team targeted criminal enterprise structures, exposing how organized crime funneled cash through legally registered businesses—and how little of it ever made its way to the IRS.

He understood that tax law, as dry as it might seem, was the one weapon that crime families couldn't easily dodge.

Money left trails.

And Fred followed them.

Strategy Over Swagger

Fred wasn't like the FBI agents who wore tailored suits and took credit at press conferences. He wasn't interested in fame. But he did understand the power of media attention—to show the public that the IRS wasn't just a desk job. And to show criminals that someone was watching.

What set Fred apart was his restraint.

He never grandstanded. He never exaggerated. He let the numbers speak for themselves. The FBI could arrest some of these guys like Al Capone for murder, extortion, prostitution, but no charges would stick. Witnesses would be afraid to say they saw someone like Capone do any of these things. That's how Eliot Ness was able to nail Capone, through his unpaid taxes. You couldn't murder an income statement, the numbers and money flow revealed the crime. So the IRS was the potent weapon against organized crime, and no other institution at that time had this power, there was no RICO law yet, no way to get these organizations or their leaders, except the IRS Intelligence Division.

But when needed, Fred made himself heard—especially when he felt the political machine above him wasn't playing fair. As his reputation grew, so did the tension between Fred and the higher-ups who wanted less heat, fewer headlines, and definitely no attention on certain "connected" targets.

Fred kept files anyway. He kept names. He kept track.

And he built cases quietly, methodically—until they were bulletproof.

The Calm Before the Collision

By this time, Fred's phone rang daily with tips—from whistleblowers, from competing bookies trying to sink rivals, even from concerned citizens. His office was stacked with folders, wire reports, subpoenas, and memos. His agents couldn't process cases fast enough.

The mob knew his name. He was on the cover of the Newspapers or in the media almost every week.

The press followed his leads.

And the IRS brass?

They started to get nervous.

He was becoming too visible. Too effective. And garnering more attention than his superiors.

And in the shadows of the White House and the Attorney General's office, that was a problem.

Fred's actual IRS Special Agent Badge that he
left in the box. U.S. Treasury Intelligence.

CHAPTER 6

Patriarca Family Targets

By the early 1960s, Fred G. Pastore had become a ghost that haunted the criminal underworld—especially in Boston's North End.

He didn't knock down doors in the middle of the night (during the day he did though!).

He didn't wear wiretaps, they weren't really a thing yet.

Fred hit them where it hurt most—on the books.

And if there was one name that kept surfacing on those books, it was a familiar name from Fred's youth and upbringing in East Boston, it was, Gennaro "Jerry" Angiulo.

Jerry Angiulo: Boston's Numbers King

Jerry ran things from 98 Prince Street, right in the heart of the North End, they called it "The Dog House", the building had a bakery that most locals thought was just a family-run business. But behind the counters and through the back door was the unofficial headquarters of Boston's illegal gambling scene—bookmaking, policy numbers, loan sharking, and more.

Jerry wasn't flashy like the New York dons.

He was strategic. Controlled. Business-minded.

He operated like an accountant—which is exactly what made him interesting to Fred.

Fred understood numbers.

And he understood how the mob used them to disappear money across dozens of cutouts and shell games.

Cat and Mouse

Fred began quietly tracking Jerry's gambling routes, his collectors, street-level runners, enforcers, and the businesses used to launder untaxed cash.

He didn't always go after Jerry directly.

Instead, he'd hit the smaller hubs—corner bars, laundromats, convenience stores—anywhere he knew Angiulo's collectors made regular stops.

These were headline-grabbing raids, where Fred and his team would break down the doors with large sledge hammers, and would smash the pinball machines, and burn the gambling slips.

They were precise. Surgical. Intentional.

Fred's goal was to make it known, that if you were not paying Uncle Sam what you owed him by collecting bets, he would come after you.

It was to chip away at the entire operation, forcing Jerry to move faster, sloppier—exposing new vulnerabilities each time.

"You could see it on the street," said one former IRS agent who worked under Fred. "After every raid, Angiulo's guys had to reshuffle their pickups. That's when Fred would strike again."

Inside the IRS Org Chart

In the Boston faction of the Patriarca family, Gennaro "Jerry" Angiulo sat at the top as Raymond Patriarca's underboss.

Below Jerry were his brothers and trusted capos—each with assigned territories and rackets. From Revere Beach to Lynn to Medford, each district had its own numbers runners, collectors, and muscle.

On the next page is an illustration of the IRS' internal org chart, showing the command structure under Jerry Angiulo.

It includes names, code names, and role. Originally assembled from a joint task force, and provided by IRS Special

This rare organizational chart of the Patriarca family was recovered by IRS CI Special Agent (retired) Jim Donahue—he literally pulled it from the top of a trash bin during an IRS Boston office renovation.

High-resolution version available at ConfidenceofTheMob.com

Agent (retired), Jim Donahue. If you want to hear about how Jim literally found this on top of a trash bin and got his hands on this org chart from the local IRS, you can listen to his interview here ConfidenceofTheMob.com/book

Going after this group wasn't a law enforcement vanity project.

This was the heart of the Boston Mafia at the time, who were making loads of money, with Jerry at the helm.

One of the targets that Fred had some documentation on was Frank Cucchiara aka "The Cheeseman". Frank was a consigliere under Raymond in the New England Mafia and supposedly represented the Patriarca crime family at the famous "Appalachin Summit" that you may have heard of where the representatives of all of the Mafia families across the nation came together to squash disputes, and share re-sources, they called them "The Commission" or in Fred's documents they called them at the time "The Syndicate". Fred and his team were watching Frank in Cuba, Boston, and anywhere else he would go.

Jerry Adjusts

As Fred's raids disrupted the Angiulo gambling circuits, Jer-ry adapted. He tightened his network, rotated locations, and occasionally shut down entire operations for days at a time.

It was costly, inefficient—and exactly what Fred wanted. I can picture my Grandfather Fred having a secret competitive respect for Jerry, as they were formidable foes, and I'm sure impressed each other with every move.

The more they shifted, the more they exposed.

And Fred kept the pressure up.

With flashy arrests.

With public takedowns.

And with un-filed tax forms, seized earnings, and disrupted cash routes.

Every time Jerry tried to stay one step ahead, Fred was already two steps into his next raid.

It was a game of chess, but only one player knew where all the pieces were hidden.

There are many other notorious names from that time period in Fred's documents. I don't want to share addresses and other details in this book, but here's a table of some of the names, cities, and what kind of illegal wagering they were suspected of being involved in.

Name	City	Type of Alleged Wagering Activity
Nicolo Angiulo	Somerville	Horses and Numbers
Donato Angiulo	Boston	Horses and Numbers
Jerry Angiulo	Medford	Horses and Numbers
John Boyle	Milton	Horses and Numbers
Abe Sarkis	Milton	Horses and Numbers
Bernard McGarry	Quincy	Horses and Numbers
John H. Williams	Winthrop	Horses
Elliott Price	Brookline	Horses
Michael Rocco	East Boston	Horses
Thomas Callahan	Dorchester	Horses
Frank Cucchiara	Watertown	Horses and Numbers
James Perlman	Waltham	Horses
Frank Vitello	West Roxbury	Horses and Numbers
Thomas J. Gandolfo	Swampscott	Horses and Numbers
Francis Santo	Worcester	Horses and Numbers
Nicholas Camerota	Springfield	Horses and Numbers

Name	City	Type of Alleged Wagering Activity
Samuel Cufari	Springfield	Horses and Numbers
Frank Scibelli	Springfield	Horses and Numbers
Andrew Pradella	Springfield	Horses and Numbers
Francis J. Sullivan	New Bedford	Horses and Numbers
Philip Buccola	Boston	N/A
Louis B. Fox	West Newton	N/A
George Gordon	Brookline	N/A
Joseph Lombardo	Everett	N/A
Pasquale Lombardo	Milton	N/A
Vincent Lombardo	Brighton	N/A
Rocco Palladino	East Boston	N/A
Michael Redstone	Boston	N/A
Harry "Doc" Sagansky	Brookline	N/A
George Sweeney	Brookline	N/A
Nathaniel Gordon	Brookline	N/A

CHAPTER 7

Bernard Goldfine

Fred was known for building cases from the ground up.

But this one? This one came from the top down—whether anyone wanted it to or not.

And it started with a flashback.

Flashback: The Iaconi Interview

It was late 1955. Fred was sitting across from Frank Iaconi, the reputed mob boss of Worcester.

Fred was there to find out what Iaconi knew about the Brinks Robbery.

The infamous 1950 heist—$2.7 million in cash and checks stolen from an armored car depot in Boston. At the time, it was the biggest robbery in U.S. history. Everyone had a theory about who was behind it. Fred thought Iaconi might know more than he was letting on. Two of the suspects in the heist were from Worcester, and if anyone knew if they had anything to do with it, Iaconi would.

But Iaconi didn't want to talk about Brinks.

Instead, he offered something different.

"You want something big?" Iaconi said. "Check out a guy named Goldfine. He's not in the streets. But he's got friends in high places. Government friends. Uniform contracts. Millions."

Fred leaned in.

"What about him?"

"He wins every bid for military uniforms. Every year. No matter what the other companies offer. You don't win like that unless you're greasing palms."

And just like that, Fred's radar shifted.

Enter Bernard Goldfine

Bernard Goldfine was a Boston-based textile magnate—born in Russia, raised in New England, and fiercely self-made. He owned mills, warehouses, and factories from Massachusetts to Pennsylvania. His business made everything from wool suits to government uniforms.

Fred ran the name through his channels.

What came back was stunning:

Goldfine's companies had won dozens of federal contracts—almost exclusively.

Despite competitors offering lower bids, Goldfine always landed on top.

He also had a habit of "gifting" expensive items to government officials—fine suits, luxury luggage, even vacations.

Fred knew this wasn't about tax evasion.

This was influence laundering.

And it needed a codename and it's own dedicated investigation.

Boston Special Project Four

Inside the IRS, Fred assembled a team and launched an official operation under the name:

"Boston Special Project Four"

This was 1957-1958, and Goldfine's books weren't sloppy—but they were layered. He had personal holdings in luxury real estate, art, and undeclared overseas assets. His factories had off-the-book workers. And his tax filings were suspiciously uniform—always consistent, always safe, always… curated. And there were always politicians, or influencers coming to his downtown Boston office. He made sure his secretary Mildred Paperman always had a box of cash in her desk so he could give a stack to whoever he wanted to, in order to get what he wanted. He was a real player, and he collected politicians like others collected baseball cards.

Fred began mapping the gifts.

One of the key recipients?

Sherman Adams—President Dwight D. Eisenhower's Chief of Staff.

<u>Some would say that Sherman Adams was the most powerful man in the world at the time.</u> Eisenhower was at the end of his second term, and was focused on other things. If you wanted something done in the administration, you went to Sherman Adams, not President Eisenhower. In fact, Adams had an office right across from Eisenhower's. Adams office door was always open and he'd be at that desk working away, or sitting down with whoever came to meet with him.

Fred uncovered that Goldfine had given Adams expensive wool suits, a Persian rug, hotel rooms, and one thing that stood out in the media, a **Vicuña Coat.** This would become known as "The Vicuña Coat Affair", this was National news. For some reason the media latched on to the Vicuña coat and ran with it. A Vicuña coat is an expensive type of fur coat.

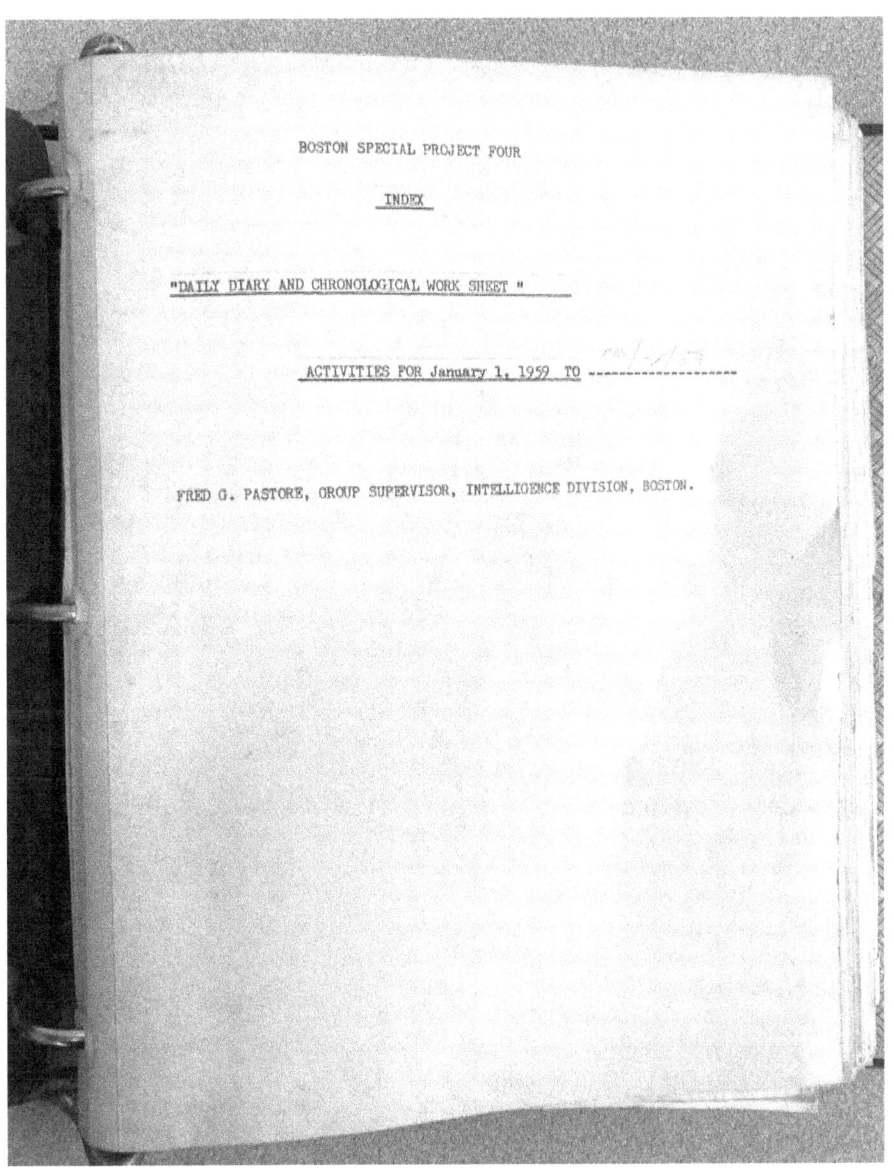

Here's the cover page of Fred's 400 page daily diary of the Goldfine investigation "Boston Special Project Four" which was in "the box" that I received from my Mom..

These
weren't just tokens—
they were influence
markers.

Adams had allegedly
intervened in regula-
tory rulings that ben-
efited Goldfine's
business. And he
made sure Goldfine
would get the military
uniform contracts every time they came up.

Fred above taking out boxes of Goldfine records out of a vehicle at the courthouse in Boston.

Goldfine would eventually have to turn his documents over to Fred, causing Goldfine lots of grief.

Fred would pursue Goldfine to provide his accounting books for his various mills and factories. Eventually the court found Goldfine in contempt as he didn't give up the records. Once Fred got the records, he was able to prove in court what Goldfine was up to. Goldfine served a short sentence, but had to give up all of his financial and business holdings.

Goldfine got ill as soon as he got out of jail, and passed away without his riches intact.

Fallout from the Top

The Goldfine-Adams scandal eventually broke into national headlines.

Fred's investigation helped ignite what would become one of the earliest post-war White House influence scandals.

Sherman Adams was forced to resign. <u>I want to reiterate and emphasize what happened here, what many considered the most powerful man in the world (Adams) at the time, was forced to resign, because Fred and his team at the IRS investigated and followed the money and corruption and it lead to the White House.</u>

69

Goldfine's contracts came under scrutiny.

Fred's name was mentioned quietly—behind closed doors—
as the "guy who wouldn't play ball."

And that's when the pressure began. It lasted for a while.

Not from the mob.

From the government.

It was now 1961

Fred compiled a memo. He made it watertight.

Then he did something few civil servants would dare:

He sent a telegram directly to the White House.

The Telegram

It wasn't long.

It wasn't angry.

But it was pointed.

Fred requested an audience—with the President of the United States (who was now John F. Kennedy), and Attorney General Robert Kennedy. He says he has a major breakthrough in the Goldfine case, and requests to meet with them at the White House within the next few days. He mentions that he will travel there on his own expense and he is awaiting their response.

Fred never received a reply.

Fred was soon offered a quiet transfer—to a downgraded role in Syracuse, New York. A demotion, disguised as a reassignment.

He refused.

He had gone too far up the chain.

And now they wanted him out of the way.

JFK & RFK Target Fred

By 1960, Fred G. Pastore had built an airtight case against Bernard Goldfine—and in the process, he'd exposed a paper trail that led straight to the White House.

But the fallout wasn't applause.

It was silence.

Then threats.

Then political pressure unlike anything Fred had experienced in his career.

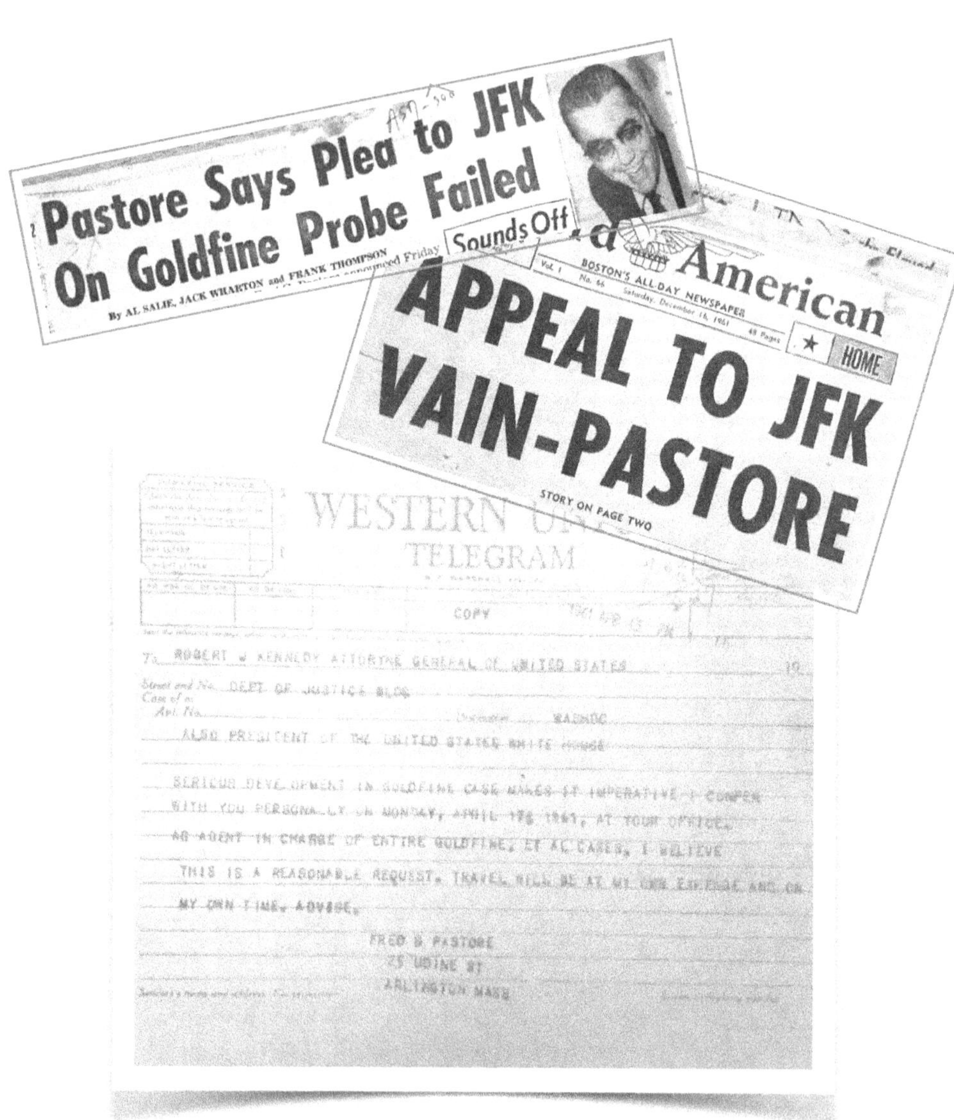

Here's a copy of the Western Union Telegram,
from the box, dated April 13th 1961 that Fred
sent to the attention of Robert Kennedy, and the
President of the United States, John F. Kennedy.
Also Newspaper headlines showing the Fred
and Kennedy clash.

The Massachusetts Web

Fred wasn't just a federal investigator.

He was a Massachusetts native.

Born and raised in East Boston.

Just like Bernard Goldfine, who had built his textile empire in the same state.

And just like the Kennedy family, who carried the pride of Massachusetts into the national spotlight.

Fred had always known that power and proximity were close cousins.

But when he started pulling threads on the Goldfine case, he realized they weren't just connected by geography—they were connected by influence.

Goldfine's gift-giving, contract-winning strategy had touched plenty of high-level officials. But Fred began to suspect that the Kennedys may have benefited indirectly, through campaign support, pressure relief, or simply looking the other way.

And that's when Fred's phone started ringing.

Robert Kennedy Turns Up the Heat

It wasn't subtle.

Then–Attorney General Robert F. Kennedy personally reached out through intermediaries, demanding that Fred identify and hand over his confidential informant that seemed to provide Fred with exclusive information on local racketeers that kept Fred ahead of everyone else.

Fred refused.

Repeatedly.

The pressure escalated—calls, visits, unofficial warnings from superiors. At one point, an internal review of Fred's own finances was quietly opened by the IRS and relayed to the Department of Justice. It was retaliation disguised as routine. In fact, Mildred Paperman, Goldfine's secretary (she also served a small sentence for being an accomplice to Goldfine's bribery), said that she had proof that Goldfine would pay Fred off. She showed the Government a check stub made out to Fred's initials **"F.G.P."**. This set Fred aback, and on defense. He said to his superiors "you're taking this allegation serious from a convicted felon, WHO I

BUILT THE CASE TO CONVICT!?. It was a wild allegation, but the IRS and the powers that be wanted Fred out of their way. Fred had kept all of Goldfine's records, and he was able to trace that check to Maine Senator, Frederick G. Payne. The same exact initials as Fred G. Pastore. What a setup! Good thing Fred was thorough, they dropped that pursuit right after Fred pointed this out. The FBI interrogation transcripts reveal Fred's defiance. When pressed, he turned the questioning back on the agents, outsmarting them at their own game.

Fred's colleagues saw the writing on the wall.

He was being boxed in.

Investigated for investigating too effectively.

The Confidential Informant

Fred never gave up the name.

He told his wife, Nina, only once:

"If I tell them who it is, they'll bury him—and then bury me."

And he was right to be cautious.

Because the person feeding Fred information about all of Jerry Angiulo and others gambling establishments, the details of the license plates who would pull up and drop off bags of betting slips and pickup bags of cash, and with bio's and description of everyone at his main gambling locations. Someone who helped Fred stay ahead of Jerry, and helped Fred garner major media attention for his raids. Someone close enough to know everything. Someone with everything to lose.

Fred kept that name in his head, the only other people who knew who he was, was President Eisenhower, and the IRS Commissioner under Eisenhower. This was the deal Fred made with the previous administration, I'll tell you two, but no one else, they agreed.

Well, no one besides Fred, Nina, Eisenhower, and his IRS commissioner knew who his informant was….until now.

As I was going through the box of my Grandfather Fred's documents that my mother left to me, I noticed one beat up brown folder titled "Confidential Informant". Inside of it were cursive notes from a yellow note pad, and other hand written notes. They were from someone who

Fred's memorandum after the FBI called him in for questioning for allegations from Mildred Paperman alleging that Goldfine had given Fred bribery money.

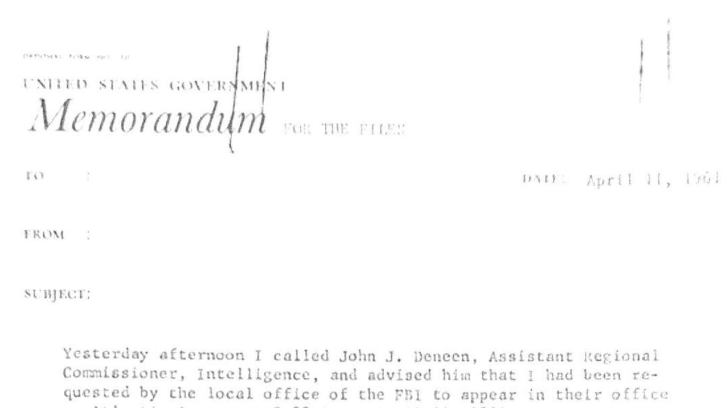

UNITED STATES GOVERNMENT

Memorandum FOR THE FILES

TO :   DATE: April 11, 1961

FROM :

SUBJECT:

Yesterday afternoon I called John J. Deneen, Assistant Regional
Commissioner, Intelligence, and advised him that I had been requested by the local office of the FBI to appear in their office
on Atlantic Avenue at 9:00 A.M., April 11, 1961.

Mr. Deneen advised me that he had taken this matter up with
Donald W. Bacon, Regional Commissioner, and that Mr. Bacon stated
it would be permissible for me to appear at the office of the FBI.

This morning at approximately 8:55 A.M., Mr. Deneen called me and
told me not to go to the office of the FBI until I heard further
from him. He later advised me that Mr. Bacon had attempted to
contact Mr. Leo Laughlin, Special Agent in Charge of the FBI for
the purpose of discussing this request his office had made upon
me, and further to suggest that his agents see me at my office.

At approximately 9:00 o'clock this morning, Mr. Deneen advised me
that Mr. Bacon could not get in touch with Mr. Laughlin, and that
I should proceed to the office of the FBI.

I appeared at FBI headquarters, 470 Atlantic Avenue, Boston, Mass.,
tenth floor, at about 9:20 A.M. I asked for FBI agent Ronald J.
Weafer and he came out and introduced me to FBI agent James J.
Strathford, Jr. I was taken to a small conference room on the
tenth floor, diagonally across from the reception room. We sat
down and I faced Special Agent Strathford, who had a block of
paper in front of him, and a pencil.

Mr. Weafer said that I was there in connection with the Goldfine
tax case; that they wanted to ask me questions about it and they
also wanted to inquire as to any possible gifts or gratuities which
I may have received. At this point Agent Strathford told me that
it was their policy to take all my statements down in longhand and
then they would prepare an affidavit from it which I would be asked
to sign. Agent Strathford told me I would be put under oath and he
also at this point advised me of my constitutional privileges under
the fifth amendment.

Page 1 of 3 of the memo.

Fred's memorandum after the FBI called him in for questioning for allegations from Mildred Paperman alleging that Goldfine had given Fred bribery money.

I asked FBI Agent Strathford who had requested that I be interviewed and he told me some one in the Department of Justice. Agent Strathford also told me that I was there voluntarily. At this point I told the agents that I was not there voluntarily but that I had appeared there at their request merely as a courtesy from one Government official to another. Secondly, I told them I wanted to know what person in the Department of Justice had requested that I be interviewed in connection with the Goldfine case. I also told the agents that any information they wanted from me concerning the Goldfine case could not be discussed by me because it would be a violation of Section 7213 of the Code, which provides for dismissal from the Service, imprisonment and fines for disclosing unauthorized information. I also told them any information they got from me concerning the Goldfine case would also be a violation of regional memoranda elaborating on Section 7213 of the Code. I asked the agents if the allegations concerning me had been made in writing or under oath. The agents told me that the allegations concerning me were not made under oath and were not in writing. I told the agents that since the allegations concerning me were not in writing and were not under oath and apparently came from Mildred Paperman, who had pled guilty to tax evasion charges, who also pled guilty to felony charges concerning Strathmore Woolen Company and is presently awaiting sentence and who is nothing but a common bum, that I would not make any statements ; under oath to refute the allegations which had not been made under oath.

I told them I would be happy to appear before any judicial body such as a grand jury to answer any questions concerning the Goldfine case, but that I certainly was not going to answer under oath any allegations about me that were not made under oath. I also told them that so far as discussing the results of the Goldfine investigation that I would not do so unless I received an appropriate letter from Washington advising me that I would not be held criminally liable for any disclosure I made that might violate Section 7213 of the Code. The agents told me that I could call Mr. Bacon who would give me the necessary waiver. I told them that in my opinion Mr. Bacon did not have the authority to circumvent Section 7213 of the Code and that I wanted the authority from someone in Washington.

I also told them that I was one of the key witnesses at the criminal contempt trials of Mildred Paperman and Bernard Goldfine and that as a result of my testimony and that of some of the other agents in the case Mildred Paperman and Bernard Goldfine were held in criminal contempt and sentenced to jail by the Court. I also told them that

Page 2 of 3 of the memo.

Fred's memorandum after the FBI called him in for questioning for allegations from Mildred Paperman alleging that Goldfine had given Fred bribery money.

every investigation arising out of the Goldfine case resulted in a recommendation for criminal prosecution. I also told them that any further interviews with me once they obtained the necessary clearance I requested as described above would have to be made at 55 Tremont Street and not at their office.

The agents said that they expected a general denial from me anyway in connection with the questions they wanted to ask, but I told them it was a question of principle with me, that I had devoted 21 years of my life to this case and I certainly resented having to appear there to testify under oath concerning charges which I believe to have been made by Mildred Paperman which were not made under oath or in writing.

Fred C. Pastore
Group Supervisor

Page 3 of 3 of the memo.

was on stakeouts, and tailing gamblers as they drove around the city. These were detailed notes from Fred's confidential informant. I handed these notes to my cousin Bobby, and almost immediately he said "this is my father's writing!". I said "no way!". You could see the emotion come out of Bobby's soul. His hands trembling, his eyes tearing up, he had to take his glasses off to wipe the tears with his fingers. When he realized that his father wasn't only an ex-military marksman and "housewares salesman", he was working with his brother Fred to take down the Boston Mafia. He was Fred's secret weapon! You could see the sense of pride in Bobby. Bobby was certain that the writing was his father's, but we had to confirm it. He asked his brother "Freddy", who is named Fred Pastore just like his uncle Fred, and also their mother Rita. Undoubtedly it was confirmed by Rita that this was her husband Giulio's handwriting. But she said he wasn't an informant. Giulio had never told her. Unfortunately we lost Rita and Giulio a few years ago, I remember Rita's smile and how she was always so nice to me and my brothers and sisters.

Fred's brother Giulio being his informant made so much sense after we pieced this 50 year old mystery together. Someone Fred would never give up, his own blood, someone who sacrificed for Fred to be where he was in his career, and a man who did much for his country, his brother Giulio. The two brothers from East Boston who came up from nothing and only had each other and a few friends in

81

those streets. See the letter in this chapter where the FBI tried to get Fred to give up his informant,

Fred protected that informant with his life and says *"he's a family man who's done much for his country, his life and his families life would be in danger if it was known, **and they would be marked for death."***

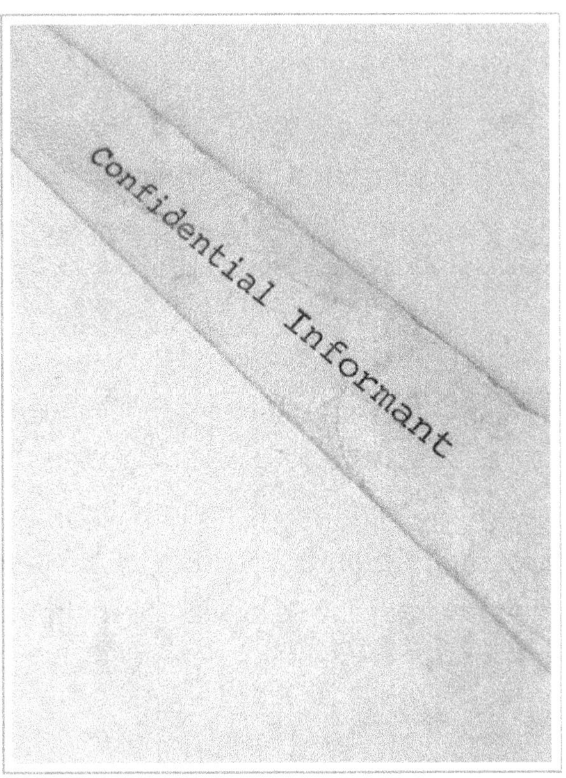

The actual folder titled "Confidential Informant" from "The Box"

Bobby, Giulio's son, tells a story about how he was playing in his front yard in Medford Massachusetts when he was a kid, in the early 1960's, a guy shows up at his house, gets out of his car, and walks up to the house. He has his car keys in his hand, and he scratches three x's on the siding of the house. The man never said a word, Bobby has no idea who that was, but it most likely had to do with his father being Fred's informant. It never made sense to Bobby until now.

Two other documents that I handed over to Bobby that were in the "Confidential" folder mentioned his father Giulio. They validate our theory that he was Fred's confidential informant.

The first letter dated August 14th, 1961, is from Philip T. Gallo, Deputy Chief of Police in Charge of the Detective Bureau in Revere Massachusetts, it is addressed to John C. McGrath, Chief of the Medford police department. It states that Giulio, who was a resident of Medford showed an identification card to one of his detectives indicating that he was a "Special Police Officer" in Medford.

Fred's letter to the commissioner of the IRS, protecting his pact with his confidential informant.

October 9, 1961

MEMORANDUM TO: Chief-Intelligence Division
                  Boston, Massachusetts

          In re: Confidential Informant

In a memorandum dated October 5, 1961 you requested the identity of
the confidential informant whose mileage and out-of-pocket expenses
have been included in my expense vouchers from February 1960 to July
1961, inclusive. These expenses fluctuate from a low of $21.60 for
the month of February 1960 to a maximum of a $100.00 a month in
1961, through July.

This confidential informant has been responsible for forty-seven
arrests in the Boston District, the seizure of twenty-eight automobiles, $23,400.00 in currency, and gambling records resulting in
the assessment of $1,200,000.00 in excise taxes, penalties and in-
terest.   These statistics include the smashing of three lay-off
syndicated groups in Revere, Massachusetts including two persons
who are now on the Organized Crime Drive list for a saturation type
investigation.   These figures do not include the additional revenue
involved in criminal income tax cases now being developed against
eight racketeers.   The latest success of this informant is the con-
viction by plea of Carmello Cocoa, whose activities were the subject
of extensive testimony by Commissioner Caplin before the McClellan
Committee in Washington during August 1961.   In no instance has the
confidential informant filed a claim for reward, nor has he furnished
any data since August 1961.

When this informant first approached me about providing information
concerning extensive wagering tax violations in Boston and Revere,
Massachusetts, he requested that if he provided the Internal Revenue
Service with information it would be done solely on the basis that
his true name would not appear in the records of any governmental
agency, including the Internal Revenue Service; and in addition, all
he wanted was mileage reimbursement and out-of-pocket expenses in-
curred while keeping certain syndicated operations under observation.
Before I made any agreement with him, I consulted with you, and later
I discussed the matter personally with the District Director, and you
both agreed that it would not be necessary for the District Director
to have the name of the informant in his files, so long as you and I
were satisfied that the informant did exist, and that he was per-
forming a valuable service.   It was further agreed that the identity
of the informer did not have to be known to anyone other than myself.
A memorandum of this conference with the District Director is attached
as Exhibit A.

Page 1 of 4.

In re: Confidential Informant

It was on the basis of this approval from my superiors that I promised the informant that his name would be known only to me, and that it would not appear in any government files.

The use of confidential informants in racketeer investigations is well recognized by the Attorney General of the United States and by the Commissioner of Internal Revenue.   Both Manual Supplement 94 RDD-1 and Manual Supplement 94 G-4, describing procedures in Organized Crime Drive cases and Major Racketeer cases, stress the use of paid informants. As Racketeer Liaison Officer for the Boston District, acting under an appointment of the District Director dated May 31, 1960, I am responsible for carrying out the program described in Manual Supplement 94 G-4 dated April 29, 1960 entitled Program and Procedures in Major Racketeer Cases, Exhibit B.   Section 9.01 of this Supplement provides that undercover agents and paid informants will be used by the Intelligence Division in investigating racketeer activities encompassing any attempt to evade taxes (income, wagering occupational, wagering excise, etc.) coming under the District Director's jurisdiction. Furthermore, the special agent's handbook and the Intelligence Division Manual stress that special agents will not renege on promises made to informants, and that their identity will be protected; otherwise, physical injury or even death may result to them from such disclosure.   And Treasury Department policies enunciated in the summer of 1961 provide that the identity of confidential informants (paid or otherwise) will not be disclosed without their consent, and that confidential informants in racketeer cases will be solicited.   I mention this merely to show how important the government considers the use of confidential informants in the fight against organized crime.

Referring specifically to my confidential informant, he told me he would give information concerning racketeer activities only if his name did not appear in any government files.   I discussed his request with the Chief, Intelligence Division, and with the District Director personally.   They both agreed that his name did not have to appear in any files and that it was satisfactory to them that

-2-

e: Confidential Informant

s identity be known only to me. I then made a promise to the onfidential informant that his identity would be known only to me, nd on that basis he provided information which was valuable to the Internal Revenue Service. He produced a lot for very little and to ask me now to submit his name to be placed in a confidential file is in effect requesting me to renege on my promise which I made in good faith as a responsible government officer.

Nonetheless, I have asked him to release me from my promise, but he refused to do so. He is a family man, who did much for his country, and he is afraid that his name will leak out and result in physical injury or death to him and his family. He is well aware that at least twenty-four criminal cases which resulted from his information have not yet been tried, involving excise taxes in excess of $1,200,000.00, and if any word got out as to his true identity, he and his family would be marked for death.

My experience in racketeer cases is that the names of confidential informants are not secret very long when they are known to persons other than the person actually receiving the information. The most recent example of this occurred before United States Commissioner Francis H. Farrell in the Federal Building Saturday morning, September 30, during a hearing involving some of the persons arrested in Boston during the raids on Massachusetts Avenue. One special agent from out of town, in the presence of the defendants, and in open court, disclosed the identity of the person who had introduced him to the bookmakers in several establishments raided, and who also familiarized them with the wagering setups in the area. The informant appeared in the office of the Intelligence Division the following Monday requesting federal protection for fear he would be physically harmed or killed as a result of the special agent publicly identifying him. In actual practice, protection either on the local or federal level, is ineffective. Other ways that the names of confidential informants can be disclosed is through the skilful cross-examination by defense attorneys who, knowing that confidential files do exist, can compel the production of the true names from the District Director's files or the Regional Commissioner's files, without obtaining it from the person who actually received the information.

Fred's letter to the commissioner of the IRS, protecting his pact with his confidential informant.

r these reasons, I cannot in good conscience, betray my confiden-
ial informant, unless he releases me from my promise which I made
nly after I had the concurrence of my superiors.

However, I do not wish to appear uncooperative or obstinate.   So
if there is any doubt as to the existence of a confidential informant, particularly in the Boston and Revere operations, I suggest
that Miss Arlyne F. Hassett, former Assistant United States Attorney
who handled all the wagering tax cases in the United States Attorney's
office, be contacted as she conversed with him several times.   Or
Special Agent John J. Daley who spoke with him on the telephone and
who also saw me conversing with him several times in Revere while we
were working there, will testify as to the existence of this informant.

Or if there is any specific information the Regional Commissioner
desires about this confidential informant, other than an outright
disclosure of his name, I shall be more than happy to sit down with
him and resolve whatever problem has arisen.

Fred G. Pastore
Group Supervisor

Page 4 of 4.

A citizen reported that he was in Revere on Ocean Avenue (Revere is right on the ocean and was a major hotbed of gambling and numbers rackets in the country at that time), and he was using his binoculars looking towards the ocean. The police questioned Giulio, and he said "he was observing women in their automobiles dressing and undressing, and that his wife is "frigid". Gallo states that he is making Medford police aware of what Giulio was up to. According to my research, Gallo may have been "on the take" to be working as a lookout for the bookies himself.

The second letter came in 3 days later on August 17th 1961, From Gallo (he only put his title on the signature, not his name this time), again addressed to Chief of the Medford police John C. McGrath. This time Gallo states that in reference to his letter that he sent 3 days earlier, he has received information that "Mr. Pastore" (not Giulio anymore....) was doing work of a confidential nature and was pledged to secrecy and under no circumstances divulge the nature of his work, even to the point of arrest. He states that he will come to Medford to explain personally if needed. We also confirmed that Ocean Avenue in Revere was where Fred made a huge gambling ring bust shortly after this time. Giulio was gathering intel, and he used his wife as his cover story.......she couldn't have been too frigid as Fred Jr. was born shortly after!

My cousin Bobby tried to think back, and he remembers a framed letter that his father kept in their garage. It was to Fred. And it commended Fred on his work for "Operation Cedar". I searched all my documents for "Operation

Cedar" and there was one result. It was a raid in Revere at 350 Ocean Ave, for an establishment owned by Carmelo Coco. Fred's team recovered a "black book" at that raid, that had names and addresses of all major racketeers in the state. It was a huge break. And my belief is that Fred gave that framed document to his brother, his secret weapon, to keep. Since Giulio couldn't formally be named in any documentation since he was a Confidential Informant.

This confirmed one hundred percent that Fred's brother Giulio was his informant. Fred kept these files in his documents so someone could decode this later on. It took over 60 years, but we figured it out! You have to understand that this is life-altering information for Bobby, his Brother Freddy and Jimmy. They had gone through their whole lives thinking Uncle Fred was this hotshot, but little did they know, their own Father was his secret weapon! Bobby recalls one time when Fred whispered in his ear,

"The President knows your Father's name". Now it all makes sense, Eisenhower knew Giulio's name, but agreed that only him, the Chief of the Intelligence Division, and Fred knew who he was. Robert Kennedy and John F. Kennedy were desperate to know his identity, Fred never gave it up. Amazing stuff.

The Demotion Offer

When pressure didn't work, politics stepped in.

Fred was presented with a career-ending ultimatum:

Accept a demotion to a lower-level Special Agent role in Syracuse, New York, where he'd be out of the action, and more importantly, out of Massachusetts where the Kennedys didn't want him snooping around and following any money trails.

The offer was designed to humiliate him. To force him to step off the National stage without a fight. To remove him from New England entirely—away from Goldfine, away from the Angiulos, away from the Kennedy backyard.

Left to Right, Fred's brother Giulio, and Fred. They are at Stella's restaurant on Fleet Street in Boston.

Fred had a turbulent week at home thinking about this with his wife Nina. Sharman and Pamela even remember putting on puppet and doll shows at home in hopes of cheering up their parents to help change the atmosphere at home. Fred felt that he dedicated 24 years to the IRS and he worked to the best of his ability, and they decide to treat him like this! He was pissed, the true grit, the little kid who knew he had to fight and stand up to the neighborhood bully, came back up to the surface, he was out for vengeance.

He refused the IRS offer to relocate to Syracuse New York.

Not only would he not relocate, he prepared for something the IRS wasn't expecting—

<u>a public reckoning.</u>

The directive letter from IRS District Director, Frank J. Cavanagh telling Fred that he was being demoted from his current supervisory position to an investigator and being reassigned from Boston to Syracuse.

The Press Conference Looms

Fred began gathering documents, statements, and clippings. He typed out one after another of revision after revision, trying to get all of his points into a two-page statement. And he also established a dossier for the internal IRS leaders that he would insist would go in his official personal file (OPF), so that historians could look back and discover the facts (which I did).

On a personal note, Fred was deliberating at home on what his next move would be. Would he really resign from the IRS, or was he going to accept this reassignment and be out of the limelight only for doing his job too well? It was tense at home, Nina and his daughters could feel it, and Fred was under a lot of pressure. After a few weeks, he made his decision.

He notified the press.

"If they're going to throw me out," he told a colleague, "I'm not going quietly. The public deserves to know what they're doing."

25 Udine Street
Arlington 74, Massachusetts
December 4, 1961

District Director Of Internal Revenue
174 Ipswich Street
Boston, Massachusetts.   Attn: Chief, Intelligence Division.

Dear Sir:

In a letter dated November 21, 1961 District Director Frank
J. Cavanagh advised me that effective December 10, 1961, I
will be reassigned from Boston to Syracuse, New York, at no
change in salary, $11,675.00, although I will not have the
position of a Group Supervisor, but that of a field agent.
In addition, since my reassignment to non-racketeer investigations in September 1961, I have not been eligible for overtime pay or premium pay which over a twleve months period
will approximate $920.00, considering present operating plans
in this field.

I have decided, in the best interests of my country, my family
and myself, not to accept the reassignment to Syracuse, but to
resign effective the close of business Friday, December 15, 1961,
and you may consider this letter to be the two weeks notice
required by Section 1882.1 of the Manual. My reasons for resigning, as required by this same Manual section, are that the
reassignment was not made in good faith but was motivated politically as retribution for my vigorous investigation of Bernard
Goldfine, his family, his secretary, his numerous interlocking
corporations and other taxable entities, and as retribution for
plans I submitted for using the internal revenue laws as potent
weapons in racketeer and wagering tax investigations.

To support these beliefs, I request that the following records of
the Intelligence Division, Internal Revenue Service, Boston, be
associated with my personnel file so that historians can determine
whether my conduct in either the Bernard Goldfine investigation
or other sensitive case area, or in the racketeer and wagering
tax areas were at any time other than in the best interests of
the Government or other than for the good of the Service.

Fred responds to Cavanagh in writing, telling him
that he is refusing the reassignment and will be resigning from the IRS instead. He says he believes this is
political retribution for the Goldfine case and not made
in good faith by the IRS.

The IRS Intelligence Unit had never seen anything like it.

A supervisor going on record.

Calling out the Justice Department.

Accusing the Kennedy administration of political retribution.

Fred announced that immediately, he was opening up his
own "Tax Fraud Defense Firm" right across the street from
the IRS. He was open for business, and he had a chip on his
shoulder, more like a boulder. Again, this is that cockiness,
and willingness to fight back against the neighborhood bully
that he learned in his youth in East Boston.

Montage of Newspaper headlines of Fred's success and clashes while at the IRS and with the Kennedys, etc.

And behind it all, the truth Fred refused to surrender.

That one name.

That one informant (we now know it was his brother Giulio, but the Government was desperate to know).

Still unknown to JFK, and RFK. Still safe. Still powerful.

Fred had told the media before his press conference that he was going to reveal a list of corrupt police officers and politicians in Boston when he would step to the podium. Fred never released the list. Fred's daughter Pam said that someone spoke to Fred, someone from the Government and said "it's probably not a good idea if you release that list".

Fred at his famed press conference.

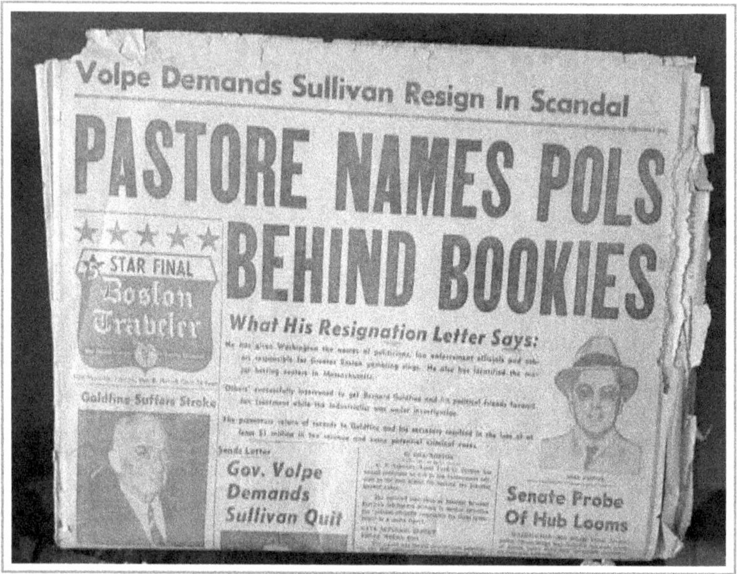

This headline has Fred's explosive resignation announcement, it also has Goldfine on the same page related to him having a stroke in jail. This was in "the box".

A vague threat. In my opinion, Fred used this list as an insurance policy. He kept the list hidden….in the box…..and he never revealed that list. I have that list. In order to not ruin any family legacies, that list will remain private.

During this tumultuous time for Fred and his family, his wife Nina said that she always felt followed when her and her daughters went shopping in downtown Boston. And my Mother Sharman said that they always had the shades drawn in the house. They were told there were men in cars across the street watching them. They couldn't play outside in their yard, it was too uncomfortable.

The fear was palpable. Nina's dentist in Medford later recalled her sitting in his chair, a family friend and great man, whispering that she believed the Kennedys had put out a hit on her husband Fred.

Fred had hit that pivotal moment in one's life where the walls feel like they are closing in, you have nowhere to turn, you either fight, or flight. Fred chose to fight, and he had the courage and grit to win, even with his family and himself in immense danger.

You can listen to Bobby Pastore talk about his story and getting emotional reading the letter about his father on our companion podcast.

Listen to Bobby talk about it here:

ConfidenceofTheMob.com/book

Or point your mobile device camera here to hear audio stories, interviews, and to see full size documents from this chapter.

CHAPTER 9

We're Going Into Business

When Fred walked out of the IRS building for the last time, he didn't walk away defeated.

He walked away ready.

He had spent over two decades investigating fraud, tracking untaxed cash, and writing internal IRS procedures. He had trained agents, testified before Congress, taken down gambling empires—and along the way, learned every weakness in the system.

Now he was ready to use that knowledge for the other side.

The Consultant Nobody Wanted You to Have

Fred opened a private accounting and tax advisory firm right across the street from his office at the IRS in downtown Boston.

But this wasn't H&R Block.

Fred specialized in tax fraud defense—the exact field he once prosecuted.

He knew how IRS agents built cases.

He knew what triggered audits, how subpoenas were drafted, and how much proof the government needed to act.

He had written some of those playbooks himself.

To his clients, Fred wasn't just a tax man—

He was a shield.

An insider who knew exactly how to protect them—legally—from the same people he used to work for.

The main challenge for Fred was, how could he get clients, and how could clients trust that the number one man at the

IRS all of a sudden made such a drastic switch in his career and life? How could they know that Fred wasn't playing them, and acting as some kind of double agent? The solution to this was one of Fred's old colleagues who had made a similar move already. Frank DiMento. Frank was US Assistant Attorney, then started his own practice with his partner Sullivan, to create the famed "DiMento & Sullivan Law Firm". Frank already had the trust of the clients that Fred was interested in gaining. Frank assured his clients that Fred was legit, and that he had switched sides due to how the IRS and the Kennedy's treated him. With Frank's assistance, Fred's business took off overnight. What was good for Frank was good for Fred and vice versa. They had the utmost tax expert in Fred, and the best Attorney in Boston in Frank, it was a win/win. A powerhouse of a duo.

Fred's first desk at his office
on 141 Milk Street in Boston

Client #1: Henry Vara

The first person that Frank brought through Fred's door as a client was Henry Vara—a towering figure in Massachusetts nightlife, business, and drinking establishments. He owned some of the most influential bars, and nightclubs at the time, and had more liquor licenses than anyone else in the state.

Henry needed someone he could trust—someone who could keep him compliant, strategic, and one step ahead of the state and federal agencies always sniffing around, and to help him keep more of his cash.

Fred was that man.

When he found out that Fred went into business on his own, Frank Dimento brought him to see Fred, he was skeptical if he was still working for the IRS or not. It was Henry's mother who convinced him to trust Fred. She met Fred, he made an impression on her, and Henry trusted his mother's judgement.

The first time they met, they were both skeptical, and both uneasy about this relationship. They were both charming, and both like to joke around and make others feel comfortable and laugh. They overcame this tension almost immediately. Henry later on made Fred the Godfather of his son Henry.

Henry also referred his friend, Irwin Chafetz, to Fred to become a client. Irwin and his business partner and friend, Sheldon Adelson (no longer with us), were the pioneers of the destination casino hotels The Venetian and The Palazzo in Las Vegas and others Globally. They are/were in the hospitality industry and rose to becoming multi-billionaires, extremely successful.

Irwin said "whatever Fred told me to do, I'd do it, whatever he said was gospel when it came to my taxes".

Left to Right: Eddy Inserra III (Me),
Irwin Chafetz, Bobby Pastore (my
cousin) in 2021
at Irwin's office.

Henry wasn't just a client. He was a referral engine.

Through him, Fred's name reached a whole new clientele:

Bar owners. Restauranteurs, Importers. Real estate developers, even Las Vegas Casino Owners, and Contractors.

And yes—former targets of IRS investigations involved in Organized Crime.

Left to Right: Fred Pastore Jr (kneeling), Bobby Pastore, Henry's Wife Patricia Nee, Henry Vara (middle), and Eddy Inserra III (me) in 2020 interviewing the late Henry.

The first two men in the top left row are Francis J. DiMento and Henry Vara, along with other family members and friends at my parents wedding.

The Unofficial Partnership: Fred & DiMento

Again, when Fred reconnected with a familiar name from his IRS years—Frank DiMento, a sharp legal mind and former Assistant District Attorney, they were a powerhouse.

DiMento had transitioned into private practice, "The Law Firm of DiMento and Sullivan", and the two men (Fred and Frank) began working together regularly on shared clients with tax issues.

Fred handled the numbers. Frank handled the cases and courtrooms.

Together, they were hand in glove—a duo that terrified prosecutors and made clients feel bulletproof.

Hear Frank DiMento describe his decades-long partnership with Fred—and how the two went from opposite sides of the courtroom to becoming trusted allies on our website.

They didn't advertise.

They didn't need to.

Fred's reputation alone filled the appointment books.

And once someone joined the inner circle, they stayed.

There was another man inside of Fred G. Pastore and associates who was doing the legwork on the tax front, while Fred was building the name and taking cases to court.

Fred had decided to reach out to his old friend from the neighborhood, Guy Spagnuolo, to see if he wanted to work at the company. Guy decided to join, and was Fred's right hand man as far as tax preparation went, and Guy was a man who could get things done. I faintly remember Guy when I used to go into the office as a child.

Myself and my cousin Bobby both had the same recollection of Guy in the office, although Bobby is 34 years older than me. We were both talking about the atmosphere in the office, who we remembered working there, and which office location we remembered and for what reasons. This was all during our conversations during our podcast. Regarding Guy, we both remembered him with his glasses on the brim of his nose, while he had piles of papers on his desk and he was always deep into one of those piles when you walked by. His office door was usually open, and if he looked up for a second, I'd get a smile from him, then he'd dive back into those papers. Guy was the workhorse regarding tax preparation. When Guy and Fred were young, they split up, Fred went to work for the IRS, while Guy had gone to the armed services, then ended up at the Post Office. He was assistant to the superintendent of the Back Bay in Boston. You can imagine that Guy had to be meticulous and organized, working at that level in the Post Office.

It was destiny that Fred and Guy would learn and hone their skills in the decades before they decided to work together again and make a name for themselves.

Fred put the right people in the right positions, even himself, because Fred didn't just do the work—he understood the game.

And he played it better than anyone.

Here's Fred at his desk at his second office at 1 Court Street in Boston, this picture says it all.

Pencil in hand, notes hanging in front of him, pens in his pocket, family photos facing him, a big leather executive chair, expensive glasses, gold ring, manicured nails, a look on his face like he was on a mission, focused, prepared, dialed in….the IRS was in trouble.

"Fred G. Pastore and Associates" was in business. The number one weapon trained and dedicated to taking down racketeers for the IRS, had now turned against them. Fred's Son-in-Law Sandy Kennedy (not related to JFK or RFK), married to his daughter Pamela, worked for Fred and said "Everyday his mentality was, what can we do today to beat the IRS?".

$$C + R = J$$

On his desk, Fred had a plaque with a cryptic equation:

$$C + R = J$$

It stood for:

Cooperation + Records = Jail

He used it as a warning—and a rule of thumb.

If you decided to **cooperate** with the IRS and you had **records**, and the IRS could line them up, you were cooked.

But if you were smart? If you followed Fred's guidance? You could stay clean, stay profitable, and stay out of handcuffs.

113

From the famed "Empire Room" at the Waldorf Astoria in New York City.

Found in "The box", various mementos from Fred's family nights out at the fancy, Waldorf Astoria.

Left to right seated at the table is Sharman, Fred, Nina, & Pamela Pastore at the Empire Room at the Waldorf Astoria in New York City having dinner & dancing.

It became his signature philosophy.

One that his clients—and even some of his old colleagues—repeated like gospel.

Fred would travel throughout the United States on a speaking circuit where he would go to Elks clubs, Churches, Kiwanis, and in front of many other groups. He'd reveal his formula of C+R=J and from what I've heard his speech was quite entertaining. Fred's speech was titled:

"The Internal Revenue Service Wants you".

1. How tax evaders get caught!
2. Why moderate size businesses are easy prey for the tax investigator!
3. Pitfalls created by keeping books and records longer than required by regulations!
4. Twelve practical rules entitled "How to Live Happily Ever After With The Internal Revenue Service"!

Fred didn't only represent underworld figures, he also represented "the little guy" when the little guy had big tax problems.

One of Fred's clients was a man named Frank Guiffrida, who was the founder of "The Hilltop Steakhouse" in Saugus Massachusetts. Believe it or not, the Hilltop was the highest-grossing independent restaurant in the United States during the late 1970's and throughout the 1980's. The waitstaff at the Hilltop were getting bothered by the IRS for not reporting their tips correctly or something like that. Fred took their case, and ultimately won and greatly helped the staff there. There are many stories like this throughout Fred's career, for this book, I am highlighting some of the big names of the time, but wanted to mention that Fred had hundreds of clients across all walks of life.

Listen to Henry Vara, Frank DiMento, Irwin Chafetz, Sandy Kennedy and others talk about C+R=J here::

ConfidenceofTheMob.com/book

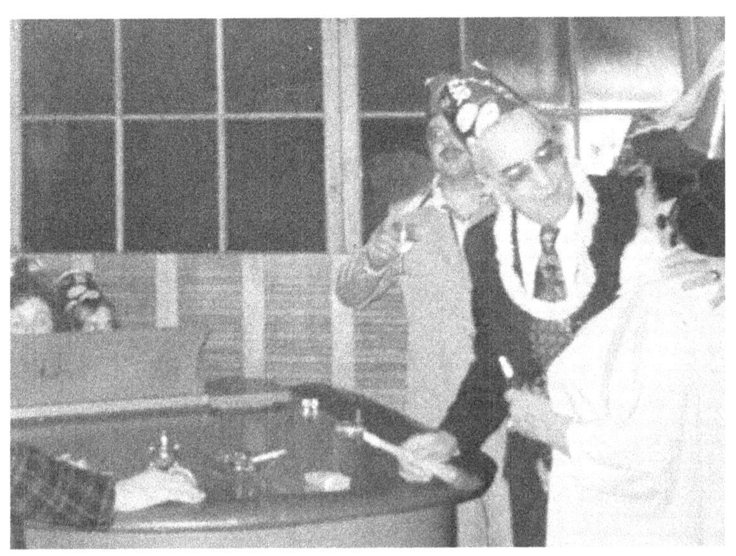

Fred and Nina caught in the moment celebrating at a Hawaiin themed luau party sometime in the 1970's.

Fred, Nina, Sharman, and Pamela enjoying life.

CHAPTER 10

Family, Friends, & FAMILY

Fred was a giant in the professional world, but at home, he was just Dad—or "Uncle Freddy" to his nephews. He cherished his role as a Father and Uncle. The feeling of togetherness and family that Fred brought to Sunday dinner, family vacations, and the little routines made the Pastore household feel like a fortress of love.

But not everyone around the dinner table was family by blood.

Sunday Dinners & The Core Crew

If you were around on Sundays, you knew the sight of Nina's famous antipasto, and the smell of her spaghetti with lobster sauce meant the day would revolve around food, laughter, and conversation that drifted from politics to business to memories of East Boston.

Fred would sit at the head of the table, usually wearing slacks and a white undershirt with suspenders, holding court while his daughters Pamela and Sharman played with their cousins Bobby and Freddy in the TV room, while Nina was in the kitchen. The occasional "old friend from the neighborhood" would sometimes swing by.

Sometimes those friends had thick gold rings, tailored suits, and arrived in Cadillacs. Other times, they were son-in-laws or other people in close proximity to some of Fred's clients that came to share info and show respect as well.

One of them was affectionately called "Uncle Nick", this was Jerry Angiulo's brother, Nick Angiulo, though no one could quite place how he was related. But on one occasion Uncle Nick brought a puppy as a gift for Sharman and Pamela. Jerry and his brothers were now Fred's clients and he would advise them on how to legally setup their businesses in order to keep more of their income and keep the IRS off their backs, and them out of jail for the next 25+ years!

They never came empty-handed.

Imported cheeses. Cakes. Boxes of Florida oranges. Rare cigars. Bottles of scotch with Italian labels.

Fred never flaunted it—but the gifts said plenty.

Trips to North Conway, and the Hawaii Jeweler

Despite his heavy workload, Fred made time for family trips.

North Conway, New Hampshire, was a favorite weekend getaway—cool mountain air, cozy inns, and quiet moments where he could just be a husband and father. Sharman remembered how Fred would hold her hand through the winding roads as a child, pointing out mountains and old buildings, telling stories he'd probably made up just to keep things fun. They'd also go up to Lake George in New York where Fred had gotten horses for Sharman and Pamela.

Ironically, once Fred ended Sherman Adams career, Mr. Adams went back to his roots working in the lumber industry back in North Conway. He ended up opening up a ski resort as well, and at the top of the summit on the tallest

121

mountain in the White Mountains, is called "The Sherman Adams Summit Building". It's amazing to me that they both ended up loving the same small town in the Mountains after all that drama.

And then there was that trip to Hawaii. Somewhere between the beaches and luaus, Fred and Nina stopped into a high-end jeweler.

She left with a diamond bracelet.

He paid in cash. Remember this story, as we reference it later.

A Blended World

Fred's home was a hub of both warmth and quiet power. Friends became clients. Clients became friends. Some stayed for dinner. Others met Fred only once—in his office, behind closed doors, their entire future depending on his advice.

He kept a small notepad on the end table next to his recliner—always ready to jot something down.

The Pastore's had financial security, no question.

But what they also had was something rarer: respect.

From neighbors. From business leaders.

And, yes—from men who most people wouldn't dare make eye contact with in public.

Fred wasn't loud.

He wasn't flashy.

He was trusted.

And that trust meant that the line between family and "FAMILY" was sometimes hard to define.

CHAPTER 11

98 Prince Street

Every Friday night, Fred would take Nina and their daughters into Boston's North End—the old Italian neighborhood packed with the scent of garlic, fresh bread, and pastry. It was a ritual. A tradition. And for the Pastore's, it felt like going home.

Fred, Nina, Sharman, and Pamela would pile into the car and drive in together. The streets were narrow, the sidewalks buzzing with vendors and old timers. Fred would tip the valet—or sometimes just double-park—and they'd head for Prince Street.

They always stopped at the bakery first.

From the outside, it looked like a hundred others in the North End. A glass case full of cannoli and biscotti. A bell above the door. Smiling faces behind the counter. But anyone who spent enough time on the block knew:

This bakery was more than meets the eye.

The Back Room

Fred would always greet the staff politely, shake a few hands, then disappear into the back room. It was never more than fifteen, twenty minutes. Nina would sit by the window with the girls, having a cannoli or lobster tail and pretending not to notice the men who came and went through the side door.

No one asked questions.

No one needed to.

This was 98 Prince Street—the base of operations for Gennaro "Jerry" Angiulo, the city's undisputed king of illegal gambling.

Fred had raided Jerry's operations for years.

And yet, here he was, back in the neighborhood, every Friday.

He wasn't there to play cards.

He wasn't there for favors.

He was there because he knew the rules—and the value—of showing face. And Jerry would only leave the North End to meet with a handful of people.

Jerry respected that.

And Fred respected the boundaries.

A Public Private Life

After the back room conversation, Fred would return like nothing had happened. He'd buy a bag of cookies for the kids, some biscotti, a loaf of bread to take home, and lead the family to the fruit market on the way back to the car to get some fresh fruit for the week.

Fred was more like an expert tax consigliere.

In this transcript, Jerry Angiulo's lieutenant, Peter Limone, mentions Fred by name, asking Jerry how Fred advised him to take the 5th amendment in court in 1964 in connection with the Indian Meadow Golf Course and Country Club in Worcester MA.

To the outside world, it looked like a quiet family outing.

To those in the know, it was something else entirely.

Fred wasn't just visiting the North End neighborhood.

He was staying visible. Advising.

Letting certain people know he was still paying attention.

He didn't need protection.

He didn't need to flex.

His very presence—calm, deliberate, steady—was enough.

Everyone Knew, But No One Said

Over time, Sharman came to recognize the rhythm of the visits. She understood, even as a child, that when her father stepped into the back of the bakery, he was doing something important—but private. The brown envelope he would come out with, he never discussed it afterward. Never bragged. Never explained.

And that silence said more than any story ever could.

Even years later, when Fred had gotten sick and Jerry's empire had begun to crumble under its own weight, no one in the family ever forgot those Fridays.

The North End.

The bakery.

The back room.

And Fred, always in control.

As Fred's visits to Prince Street continued, his health began to fade...

CHAPTER 12

Fred's Final Years

In the final chapter of Fred Pastore's life, the spotlight faded—but his presence never did.

By the 1980s, the raids were behind him. The suits were worn softer. His voice, still firm, carried more wisdom than fire. And while his body began to slow, his mind never did. He remembered dates, numbers, and names like they were etched in granite.

He was still Fred.

Just a quieter version.

The Mountain House

Fred and Nina had always loved New Hampshire.

They built a mountain house in North Conway—a peaceful place far from the North End, far from the pressure and noise of Boston. He'd sit outside in the mornings with a cup of black coffee, his newspaper, breathing in the stillness.

Family would visit.

Laughter would echo off the trees.

He was no longer running operations or advising clients.

Now, he was Grandpa. Dad. Fred.

And he loved every minute of it.

Left to Right, Eddy Inserra II (My Dad), Sharman Pastore (My Mom), and Fred Pastore. They are at the property in North Conway New Hampshire.

The Condo Near the Family

Eventually, Fred and Nina also bought a condo closer to his daughter Sharman and husband Eddy II (my parents) in Woburn Massachusetts. They wanted to be near the grandkids—to make memories, not just tell stories. But don't get the wrong idea, this wasn't a simple townhouse, it was a 3 story Condo/Townhouse and they had white carpets on the top two floors, fully finished in law apartment in the basement and a full Sauna and Jacuzzi room as well. I remember thinking as a kid that the walk-in closets on each floor could have been bedrooms themselves. We'd literally play in the closets all day. I remember Fred's electric shoe buffer, I would turn it on and try to hold on to the red spinning buffing wheel while it spun. If you looked at it from the outside, it looked like a regular townhouse, but once you went inside, you could see how much work and customization was done.

But Fred's health was changing.

His energy dimmed.

And one day, after a doctor visit no one really talked about, the family knew: he was sick.

It moved fast.

Too fast.

133

A Father's Legacy

Fred and Nina eventually moved into the home where their daughter Sharman lived in an in-law apartment on the first floor.

Her husband—Eddy II, my Father—took care of him. Every day. I remember him changing the medical patches on his skin. Fred was frail, far from the man he had been physically just a few years earlier.

My Father would help Fred with the little things: light bulbs, groceries, errands.

Fred, who could write thousand-page fraud reports and memorize banking codes, but couldn't fix a leaky faucet. He'd chuckle about it, shrug, and call for help. And my dad would always answer.

He never once complained.

Because he loved Fred like a father.

"Your Grandfather was the smartest man I ever knew," my father used to say to me. "But he couldn't change a lightbulb if his life depended on it. That's how you knew he was a genius." Meaning that one characteristic with many geniuses is that they are experts at what they do, but anything outside of that, they can't do, and lack those skills.

They worked side-by-side for years. Fred trusted him with the books, the firm, the secrets.

It wasn't just a professional bond. It was love.

The Office Meeting That Changed Everything For Me

One memory stands out.

I was just a kid, visiting the office to hang out with my father when a man was in the conference room with my grandfather Fred—I was 5 years old, I was playing at my father's desk with a toy car. My father's office had a side door which connected to the conference room with this long desk, to me it was a mile long, and at the far end was my

Grandfather Fred with another man. He said "Eddy, come here", and I went over, I was skeptical of the man. My Grandfather said "right here" pointing at his feet, so I went closer. He told me to shake the gentlemen's hand, I did. The man said to Fred "is this Eddy's son?", Fred said "yes. Eddy go back in your dad's office and play".

I didn't understand it then, but later I'd learn who he was: Steve "The Rifleman" Flemmi, notorious hitman of the infamous "Winter Hill Gang" and, a name that would go on to make headlines in mob trials and federal indictments.

Another story of Steve Flemmi that my father loved to tell was, one day Steve came into the office. In the lobby where the receptionist was, Steve asked the receptionist, Elaine, if he could use the phone on her desk. She denied him the phone and said it was office policy that no clients could use their phones. Steve got so angry, he screamed down the hall for my father, he said "Eddy get out here!". My father came out and saw Steve's eyes, he said he looked like a totally different person, filled with anger. He said to my father, "She won't let me use the phone, YOU GET RID OF HER, OR I FUCKING WILL!!". My father calmed him down and brought him in the office to use another phone. Shortly after this Elaine was fired, but it sounds like things could have been much worse.

The Wake

When Fred passed in 1988, it felt like the foundation of our family shifted, because it did. I was only 8 years old, but you could feel it, Fred was the Patriarch.

The wake was packed.

Not just family. Not just friends.

But men in suits. Former clients. Businessmen.

Quiet types. Powerful types.

Frank DiMento, his old courtroom counterpart turned closest professional ally, and dear friend, delivered the eulogy. It was heartfelt, respectful, and quietly powerful.

Frank shared the story that he learned what he calls a "life lesson" from his friend Fred, he calls it "Sharman's Doll". Decades later, Frank DiMento still told the story of 'Sharman's Doll' with a catch in his voice.

The story starts one late afternoon in Post Office Square in Boston, Fred and Frank were working on a case. They were in an office building. They had a big case that they were expected to be in court for the next morning, and they have tons of work to do before then. They start working, and they are in the zone, when suddenly Fred looks at his watch, notices it's 4pm, and starts to pack up to leave. Frank says "Fred what the hell are you doing, we have a lot of work to do, where are you going?". Fred replies "I've got to go" and Frank says "what are you talking about, we have this case to prepare for", Fred says "I've got to get a doll for Sharman before the store closes". Frank says "You can get her five dolls after the case is over, what are you talking about?....**A DOLL??**". Frank is talking to Fred like he's lost his mind. Fred says to Frank calmly "tomorrow is Sharman's birthday, she wants a doll, I promised her a doll, so I need to stop working to go get the doll." Frank stood there in astonishment, he didn't get it at the time, how you could prioritize anything, especially a toy for your kid over work? But Fred understood that family is the most important thing in most peoples lives, for sure in his. Frank says, it was a life lesson for him, and he wishes that he did more things like that in his life, and prioritized family over work. Frank is 98 years old today, and he still tells this story among a few others that were life lessons that he learned from Fred.

My mother Sharman recently had her 70th birthday, we surprised her with a party at my Godparent's house (Al and Gemma Valente), and I invited Frank to the party. This is how impactful the "Sharman's doll" story was to him. He showed up with a custom made doll, that he had to custom order himself at a store, that said "Sharman" on it as a gift for my mother. He delivered "Sharman's Doll" to "Sharman". His hands were shaking when he gave it to my mom, the look of pride on his face was shining through as he looked into my mother's eyes when he gave it to her, and he said in a choked up voice "It's Sharman's doll".

It was extremely impactful for me to see and meant so much to my mother and myself.

Hear Frank DiMento recall this story and others here:

ConfidenceofTheMob.com/book

*Or point your mobile device
camera here to hear audio
stories, interviews, and to
see full size documents from
this chapter.*

Frank DiMento, Sharman (Pastore) Inserra, and Sharman's Doll at her 70th
Birthday party in 2024.

CHAPTER 13

Finding Millions of Dollars

Fred was never loud about his money.

He didn't flaunt it.

He didn't drive flashy cars or wear gold chains.

But he always had enough—

Enough to take Nina out for dinner any night she asked,

Enough to send the family to North Conway without blinking,

Enough to take his brother Giulio and his family out to a restaurant on the way back from North Conway.

Enough to walk into a Hawaii'n jeweler and pay in cash.

Still, no one really understood just how much he had saved and invested—

Until after he died. My grandmother Nina thought she would run out of money, and she didn't know what to do.

The Discovery

It started while cleaning out the town house.

My mother, Sharman, and my Grandmother, Nina, were going through drawers, cabinets, and boxes of papers. Tax forms, ledgers, old receipts—Fred had kept everything.

And then they found them:

<u>Bank passbooks.</u>

Not one.

Not two.

Dozens.

Old-school savings books from banks all over Massachusetts and New England. Each one with deposits, balances, and in some cases, bonds and certificates attached.

At first, my mom thought it was just a curiosity.

But the numbers weren't small.

So she and Nina got in the car and started driving.

Bank to Bank

They went from branch to branch—Cambridge, South Boston, The North End, Woburn, Lowell—sometimes with nothing more than a name and a dusty account number.

And one by one, the balances added up.

Fred hadn't just saved.

He had quietly built a fortune.

Meticulously.

Privately.

Legally.

Some accounts had stock dividends.

Others had U.S. savings bonds.

The man who built his career advising others on how to protect and preserve their money—had done exactly that for his own family.

No One Knew

Nina was shocked.

She'd always known Fred was "comfortable."

But she had no idea just how methodical he'd been.

He had never spoken about these accounts.

Never bragged.

Never explained.

And yet, he had left behind a detailed paper trail—

Just in case.

Because Fred was always thinking three steps ahead.

Even after death.

The Money Was Spent, Enjoyed, Wasted... and Remembered

In the years that followed, some of that money was spent wisely.

Some of it was spent foolishly.

But I remember Christmases with car loads of presents once "Nana Nina" showed up to Christmas Eve at our house. She'd pull up in her red Cadillac or silver Lincoln, beep three times, and me and my siblings would go nuts. I'd make multiple trips out to the car (along with about 5 other family members) to help bring in all the gifts. She spoiled all of her Grandkids, and was very generous and charitable.

145

My Grandmother "Nana Nina" was boisterous, outgoing, and loved by many. I remember as a kid, when we'd go out to a restaurant with her, the waitstaff would scramble and say "Nina's here!, get her table ready". I thought it was normal at the time. Nina had her own stretch limousine driver named "Tom" who would drive her back and forth from her Woburn MA townhouse to her North Conway NH home every other weekend. We'd go to the local amusement park near North Conway NH once a year when we stayed at her house. We'd pull up to the entrance gates in a stretch limousine with 9 kids and 5 adults. Again, I thought this was normal, but everyone at the gate must have been thinking "what the hell is going on here?". Things like that, Nina loved to live life to the fullest, and she shared it with her loved ones.

And some of the money—like Fred's best advice—still lives on through the people who inherited his way of thinking.

What mattered more than the cash was the realization:

Fred hadn't just left memories.

He'd left structure.

A foundation.

A final gift.

And as Sharman and Nina stood in line at the banks, signing forms, collecting statements, one thing became clear:

Fred had never stopped protecting them.

Not in life.

Not in death.

Not ever.

Actual photo of the passbooks found at my Grandmother Nina's house after Fred passed away, adding up to millions of dollars that Fred was stacking up, unknown to Nina.

CHAPTER 14

Final Impact

Some men leave behind empires.

Others leave behind cautionary tales.

Fred G. Pastore left behind something rarer:

A blueprint.

A blueprint for how to stand your ground.

For how to do the right thing when it's hard.

And for how to never back down from what you know to be true.

Fred was the star of our family—not in the flashy sense, but in the foundational one.

He built something that allowed the rest of us to rise.

Financially. Morally. Emotionally.

Hawaii'n Nina

Here's a funny story that my cousin Bobby Pastore shared with me, and I love to hear this story as well. You can listen to him tell it in the podcast.

Remember earlier in the book I said Fred bought Nina jewelry for cash in Hawaii? Here's why. Bobby and his wife Susan, many years ago went to Hawaii on vacation, they decided to go into a random jewelry shop, and Bobby bought Susan some jewelry during their trip. Bobby pulled out his credit card and gave it to the woman working at the Jewelry store. She see's Bobby's last name on his credit card. She asks Bobby "are you related to Nina?". Bobby said his jaw dropped, and after the initial shock, he said "yes, actually I am". I guess she was one of their best customers! Imagine going to the Island(s) of Hawaii, shopping at a random shop, and the woman knowing who Nina was? Pastore isn't the most common name, but there are plenty of Pastore's out there, Nina was the kind of person who made an impact when she met you. She was the best, outgoing, generous, loving, and a great Grandmother. Nina loved to shop, and this story shows that she shopped all around the world. I just can't get over the odds of this one.

C + R = J

Fred's famous formula that I mentioned earlier. Even after all these years, his old IRS formula still echoes in strange places.

<u>Cooperation + Records = Jail.</u>

I once met with a current IRS agent (now retired), his name is Jim Donahue, he's in the podcast—long after Fred was gone—and during the conversation, he said something that made me freeze.

"One of the old-timers at the IRS uses this old-school metric as a sort of litmus test. We call it C + R = J."

He had no idea where it came from.

I just smiled.

Because I knew.

Fred had coined it.

It was on his license plate.

It was engraved on his desk.

It was in every talk he gave to a client.

It was his code—and now it was government gospel.

That's me, and my Grandpa Fred, a lifetime ago, but with great memories and stories to tell.

The People He Saved

Stories still surface.

From time to time, my cousin Bobby Pastore will run into someone—an old friend, a former businessman—who says something like:

"Your uncle Freddy saved me. He kept me out of jail."

Fred didn't always brag. But his impact was undeniable.

He changed lives.

He created second chances.

And he did it all without compromising who he was.

The Box

I've mentioned this earlier, this was the box full of Fred's documents that I've mentioned throughout the book. Years after Fred passed, I was handed a box by my Mother.

It had been sitting in storage, untouched.

Inside were his files, his notes, his journals—a complete archive of his career.

It was like someone had hit "pause" on a man's life and left it waiting for me.

As I read through the hundreds of pages—typed memos, handwritten logs, court records—I realized I wasn't just uncovering my grandfather's story.

I was inheriting his mission.

That box inspired this book.

It inspired the podcast.

It might even inspire a TV series or film, if the right door opens.

Because this story isn't just about racketeers and political scandals.

It's about a man who wouldn't be moved.

A man who did his job too well, and paid the price.

And a man who, in the end, proved that truth still matters.

Explore some of the documents, and Fred's belongings from the IRS that I discover in this box, in the podcast I created about this story at:

ConfidenceofTheMob.com/book

155

My Own Journey

I work in technology now, I was inspired from my Father in that sense, he was a wiz with technology and was a pioneer in the computer space back in the day.

I've built companies, led teams, helped launch products in the world of X-ray detection and digital platforms.

I've been fortunate in many ways. But I also had to figure things out without a formal college education and limited direction. I am self-taught in everything that I do, I get that from my father.

But the structure, the grit, the instinct?

That came from Fred.

That came from a legacy built long before I was born.

But the one thing I will never forget is to take care of your family first, your immediate family, and your brothers, sisters, nieces, nephews, parents, etc. As long as they don't cross the line, never let them fall if you can help it. And that is what I do.

Because when a man like Fred walks into history, he doesn't walk out.

He leaves footprints.

And if you follow them closely enough…

You just might find yourself exactly where you're meant to be.

Stay tuned for a second book where it's strictly some of Fred's case files and other interesting documents from "The Box".

Thanks for reading.

-Eddy

CHAPTER 15

References & Documents

The Pastore Files

1. Telegram to President John F. Kennedy and Attorney General Robert F. Kennedy

Date: 1960

Context: Fred's direct message to the highest levels of American government, protesting political interference in his investigation into Bernard Goldfine.

Commentary:

Fred typed this telegram himself, refusing to let anyone else edit it. It wasn't just a message—it was a warning. The fact that he sent it to both JFK and RFK shows how close the heat had gotten to the top. He never received a reply.

2. IRS Intelligence Division Internal Memo – Boston Special Project Four

Date: 1959

Context: Launch memo for the Bernard Goldfine investigation, authored by Fred and distributed to his hand-picked team.

Commentary:

This was Fred's blueprint for a full-scale takedown. Inside are names of financial institutions, suspected shell companies, and a timeline for rolling subpoenas. This document shows the meticulous precision that became his hallmark.

3. Fred's IRS Journal Entry – Interview with Frank Iaconi

Date: 1955

Context: Entry from Fred's handwritten daily journal, detailing the now-famous conversation where Iaconi first mentions Bernard Goldfine.

Excerpt: "Mr. Iaconi stated: 'You're looking at the wrong crowd. You want to catch a real crook, check Goldfine's bid sheets.'"

Commentary:

The informality of the line makes it all the more powerful. Iaconi, a mob boss, handed Fred the first breadcrumb in what would become a national scandal. Fred had the foresight to record it all in detail.

4. IRS Organizational Chart – Boston Faction of the Patriarca Crime Family

Date: 1972

Context: This was created after Fred worked at the IRS and while he represented many of the people on the chart with their taxes at the time. But a joint task force between the IRS, FBI, and State Police put this together.

Commentary:

This chart was never meant for public eyes. It was actually being thrown away by the IRS in Boston during a renovation, Jim Donahue (IRS Special Agent, Retired) grabbed it. It reflects the key players of the Boston faction of the Patriarca Crime Family who Fred was initially targeting.

5. Fred's Personal Notes – "C + R = J" Philosophy

Date: Early 1960s

Context: Found on notepads, folders, and even scrawled into the leather of his desk blotter.

Commentary:

"Cooperation + Records = Jail" wasn't just a rule of thumb —it was Fred's signature logic. It reflected his belief that every criminal case boiled down to two things: how much you cooperated if the IRS came to you, and if you had provided them with your records.

6. Press Clippings – Fred's Federal Building Press Conference

Date: December 15, 1961

Context: Newspaper scans of Fred's public stand against the IRS and the Kennedy administration.

Headline: "IRS Official Calls Out Political Pressure – Names Kennedy in Public Statement"

Commentary:

This was the moment Fred stopped working inside the system—and started exposing it. The press conference was unprecedented. The headlines were bold. And the ripples lasted for years.

7. Audio Archives – Podcast Interviews

Format: QR Codes

Context: Companion audio interviews featured in the Confidence of The Mob.

• Henry Vara – Fred's first client.

• Frank DiMento – Fred's longtime legal partner and former ADA.

• Family Voices – Reflections from Fred's children and grandchildren.

Commentary:

These audio clips bring Fred's story to life in a way paper can't. His legacy doesn't just live in documents—it lives in the people he helped, fought for, raised, and inspired.

8. The Box

Contents: Handwritten notes, case files, surveillance logs, letters, court records, passbooks.

Commentary:

This box sat untouched for decades. Inside was Fred's life—meticulously documented and left behind as a challenge, a gift, and a spark. It was this box that led me to create this book. To build the podcast. And to push for something even bigger—a TV series or film that will carry his legacy even further.

Because stories like this don't disappear.

Not when the truth is too powerful to stay buried.

Index

A

- Adams, Sherman (Chief of Staff): 65, 67, 69, 121, 158
- Adelson, Sheldon: 106
- Angiulo, Donato: 59, 120
- Angiulo, Gennaro "Jerry": 9, 22, 23, 52–58, 59, 77, 120, 124–128
- Angiulo, Nicolo "Nick": 22, 24, 59, 120
- Apalachin National Mafia Meeting: 39, 57
- Arlington, MA: 73, 93, 95

B

- Bacon, Donald W. (Regional Commissioner): 78, 79
- Bennett, Walter "Wimpy": 22, 24
- Bioni, Larry (Ilario Zannino): 22, 24
- Black Book (Raided Mob records): 89
- Boston Federal Building: 1, 3, 157, 163
- Boston Special Project Four: 64, 66
- Brinks Robbery: 34, 61, 62
- Buccola, Philip: 25, 28, 60
- Bulger, Whitey: 29

C

- C + R = J (Cooperation + Records = Jail): 113, 117, 151, 162
- Callahan, Tommy: 25, 28, 59
- Cavanagh, Frank J. (District Director): 93, 95
- Chafetz, Irwin: 106, 117
- Coco, Carmello: 24, 84, 89
- Confidential Informant ("The Folder"): 75, 76–83, 84–87, 89, 91, 154
- Cucchiara, Frank "The Cheeseman": 57, 59

D

• DiMento, Frank (DiMento & Sullivan): 38, 41, 104, 105, 108, 109, 117, 137–139, 163, 166

• Donahue, Jim (IRS Special Agent, Retired): 56, 57, 151, 161

E

• East Boston, MA: 7–11, 14, 40, 41, 52, 59, 60, 74, 119

• Eisenhower, Dwight D.: 65, 77, 89

• Eliot Ness: 48, 159

F

• FGP Initials (Alleged Payoff Scandal): 75, 76

• Flemmi, Steve "The Rifleman": 135–136

G

• Goldfine, Bernard: 2, 5, 20, 59, 61–71, 72, 73, 75, 78, 80, 90, 95, 99, 158, 160

H

• Hilltop Steakhouse (Saugus, MA): 117

I

• Iaconi, Frank ("Gambling Czar"): 35–38, 61, 160

• Inserra, Eddy III (Author): 10, 106, 107, 156, 158

• Inserra, Edward Robert II (Eddy's Father): 132, 133–135, 156, 166

• IRS Intelligence Division: 1, 23, 24, 30, 45–50, 159, 160

K

• Kennedy, John F. (JFK): 2, 20, 70, 72, 73, 74, 89, 98, 158, 159

• Kennedy, Robert F. (RFK): 2, 49, 70, 72, 73, 75, 89, 97, 104, 158, 159

L

• Lombardo, Joseph: 23, 27, 60

N

• North Conway, NH: 121, 131, 132, 141, 145, 146

- North End (Boston): 12, 27, 34, 52, 53, 60, 119, 124–128, 131, 143

O
- Operation Cedar: 24, 88, 89

P
- Paperman, Mildred (Goldfine's Secretary): 64, 75, 78, 79, 80, 97
- Pastore, Fred G. (Protagonist): 1–18, 20, 30, 52, 61, 72–100, 102, 130–141, 148–157
- Pastore, Giulio (Brother/Informant): 1, 7, 10, 11, 81–83, 88, 89, 91, 141
- Pastore, Nina (Wife): 1, 8, 9, 14, 15, 76, 92, 94, 99, 118, 124, 130, 141–146, 148–150
- Patriarca Family: 22, 23, 25, 52–58, 59, 161
- Prince Street (98 Prince Street): 29, 53, 124–129

Q
- QR Codes (Transmedia content): 4, 101, 117, 140, 163

R
- Racket Squad: 45–51
- Raytheon Raid: 31–34
- Revere, MA: 14, 24, 26, 39, 55, 60, 83, 87, 88

S
- Sagansky, Harry "Doc": 26, 27, 28, 60
- Sharman's Doll (Historical Anecdote): 137–140
- Spagnuolo, Guy: 9, 13, 110–111
- Syracuse, NY (Transfer order): 1, 5, 71, 90, 92, 93, 95

T
- The Box (Fred Pastore Archives): 1, 3, 18, 66, 73, 77, 81, 82, 98, 99, 114, 153–156, 158, 164

V
- Vara, Henry: 105–108, 117, 163, 167
- Vicuña Coat Affair: 5, 65, 67, 72, 74, 158

W

- Western Union Telegram (1961): 1, 73, 92, 158, 159, 163
- White House: 70, 71, 72, 74, 159
- Woburn, MA: 132, 143, 146
- Worcester, MA: 35, 37, 59, 61, 128

I'd like to give special thanks to the following people for helping me dig deep into this story to make it what it is. My wife Eileen Inserra for giving me the constant support and the patience when I'd cover our kitchen counters with these documents for weeks while I put the timeline together, and while I wrote this story and recorded for the podcast. My cousin Bobby Pastore was paramount in keeping me curious to get to the bottom of some of the loose ends in the box. Without his genuine interest in this, it may have stalled out, he helped in many ways and is a partner in the podcast. My Mother Sharman Inserra (Pastore) inspired me to do this, and she has been one of the main sources of info for me in this story. Frank DiMento aka "The Original", I reached out to Frank years before I received the box in order to find out more about my Grandfather Fred. When I first met him, my impression was "wow, my Grandfather was a close friend and colleague of the type of men with this kind of stature and confidence in their career, and intelligence". Frank is a relic of my Grandfathers time that I could still tap into, at 98 years old, I admire his accomplishments in the courtroom, his storytelling, and his family for also opening up to me and my family. I'd also like to thank my younger sister Lyndsey Inserra for finding some of the key photos in this book in part of my mother's attic. Thanks to my brother Mark for always having my back and support. My sons, Eddy IV, Andrew, and nieces Skyla and Julianna for giving me a reason to get this to the finish line so their great

Grandfather's story won't just fade away. And to my own father, Edward Robert Inserra II, I miss you. My Aunt Joyce, Janis, and Bob and Annie Inserra for their constant support. Henry Vara, and a special "yo yo yo" to my cousin Fred Pastore Jr, the Valente's, all my cousins. Cousin Victor Ausilio and his family. Cousin Tommy Austin. Aaron Hain at the Mob Museum. For all the other family and friends who have supported me in this long journey, thank you.

 Born and raised in Woburn, Massachusetts, Eddy is a lifelong entrepreneur, pioneer of the "link in bio" social media space, and subject matter expert in X-ray detection technology.

After receiving a box filled with Fred's personal case files from his mother filled with government memos, and handwritten notes, Eddy embarked on a journey to uncover his grandfather's hidden legacy—a story that intertwined organized crime, political scandal, and the enduring fight for integrity.

Eddy is also the creator and host of the companion podcast, which brings Fred's story to life through firsthand interviews, archival documents, and rare historical insights. If you had ever heard of Fred, or knew him, Eddy would love to hear from you. Contact him via the website.

Today, Eddy lives in Massachusetts with his family, where he continues to build new platforms, tell powerful stories, and honor the legacies that shaped him.

Continue this story with the companion podcast, and view the full contents of "The Box", watch videos, and more at:

ConfidenceofTheMob.com

Or point your mobile device camera here to hear audio stories, interviews, and to see full size documents from this chapter.